Baby MASSAGE

Baby MASSAGE

❖

DR. ALAN HEATH & NICKI BAINBRIDGE

FOREWORD BY PROFESSOR KIM OATES,
CHIEF EXECUTIVE, NEW CHILDREN'S HOSPITAL, WESTMEAD, NSW

PHOTOGRAPHY BY JULIE FISHER

A Dorling Kindersley book

Dorling Kindersley

LONDON, NEW YORK, SYDNEY, DELHI, PARIS,
MUNICH AND JOHANNESBURG

Project editor
Salima Hirani

Art editor
Vicki Groombridge

Photographic art direction
Toni Kay

Managing editor
Susannah Marriott

Deputy art director
Carole Ash

Production controller
Joanna Bull

*This book is dedicated to all the children
and parents that have attended our
Healthy Start Clinics.*

First published in Australia in 2000
by Dorling Kindersley Pty Limited
(A.C.N. 078414445)
118–120 Pacific Highway, St Leonards, NSW 2065

National Library of Australia
Cataloguing-in-Publication data
Heath, Alan R.
Baby Massage
Includes index
ISBN 1 7403 3422 1
1. Massage for infants. 2. Massage for
infants – Pictorial works. I. Fisher, Julie.
II. Bainbridge, Nicki. III. Title.
615.8220832

Reproduced in Singapore by Colourscan
Printed and bound in China
by L.Rex Printing Co. Ltd
www.dk.com

CONTENTS

FOREWORD

——————— ❖ ———————

All babies differ – in their personalities, their responses and their rates of development. They are also similar in many ways. They all need care, love, protection, security and opportunities to learn. Parents in many cultures who massage as part of their normal baby care believe that rhythmic stroking of their baby's body helps reduce crying, enhances health and contributes to the baby's emotional wellbeing.

Whatever one believes about baby massage, there is no doubt that it meets many of a baby's needs. The gentle caressing can be an expression of love, the routine can provide a sense of security, the rhythmic touching can be soothing, and the parent can give focused attention, so strengthening the bond between parent and child. This can be especially valuable if you talk to your baby during this time so that, as well as your touch, the baby hears the rhythm and pattern of speech, laying down the groundwork for later speech development. This is particularly important for children with special needs, who often benefit from extra input to help them develop to their full potential. Massage is also an activity that fathers can do just as well as mothers.

Having a baby produces lots of enjoyment, many challenges and not a little anxiety. If you and your baby both enjoy the experience of regular baby massage, you may find that it not only soothes your baby, but that it also enhances your relationship.

Kim Oates, AM, MD, MHP, FRACP, FRCP, FRACMA, FAFPHM, DCH
Chief Executive, New Children's Hospital, Westmead,
Professor of Paediatrics & Child Health, The University of Sydney

INTRODUCTION

❖

Ｔhe therapeutic effects of massage have been used for adults for a long time, but only recently in the West has the practice of baby massage begun to gain recognition. In parts of Africa, Asia, and South and Central America, however, women have massaged their babies for centuries. Infant massage is an integral part of the help we offer our clients at our Healthy Start Clinics. At the crying, sleep, feeding, and behavior clinics, which were set up to advise and support parents experiencing difficulties with the early challenges of parenthood, we often encountered parents who avoided touching their babies because inexperience made them nervous. This led to problems since infants need plenty of positive touch to feel secure. Other parents had problems understanding their infants. If a baby cries and the parent does not know how to "make it better," the baby tends to cry even more, frustrating the parent. In this way, a pattern is set for a downward spiral. We also saw that some parents find it harder to deal with an incessantly crying baby than others, and need to find effective ways of coping.

Baby massage proved to be a practical solution to these problems. Through massaging their babies, parents gain confidence in handling them. They learn to watch and interpret their baby's reaction to touch, which sheds light on what the infant likes and dislikes, making it easier for the parents to understand him. When parents enjoy their child's reactions, and respond to them, the baby reacts too, and a positive relationship develops between them. Parents who consulted us have become visibly more affectionate toward their babies since beginning a regular massage routine, and report that their children are happier, more self-assured, calmer, cry less, and sleep better. Parents of babies who cried a lot, usually colicky babies, claim that even when massage did not calm their child, they felt better by having tried something positive, and thus felt more able to cope. These results, and the belief that all families can benefit from massage, spurred us on to write this book.

Massage can strengthen your baby's muscles and joints and help relieve the symptoms of common childhood ailments, but most importantly, it allows you to express your love for your child through touch and helps you establish a relationship with him early on in his life. As you continue to massage him through the different stages of his childhood, the loving touch you share enhances your relationship with him every step of the way, giving him the security he needs to grow into a happy, confident, and emotionally secure adult.

Nicki Bainbridge   *Alan Heath*

Nicki Bainbridge
RGN RHV B.Sc (Hons) ITEC
Nurse and Specialist Health Visitor

Dr. Alan Heath
BA (Hons) MSc PhD AFBPsS
Consultant Child Psychologist

KEY TECHNIQUES

❖

MASSAGING YOUR BABY IS A WONDERFUL THING TO DO. IT IS SO SIMPLE IN TERMS OF TECHNIQUE, YET SO POWERFUL IN WHAT IT CONVEYS — YOUR LOVE, YOUR UNDERSTANDING AND YOUR ATTENTION. THIS SECTION INTRODUCES THE BASIC TECHNIQUES AND MAPS OUT A HEAD-TO-TOE MASSAGE PROGRAMME FOR YOUR BABY. APART FROM A FEW ESSENTIALS, THERE IS NO 'RIGHT' OR 'WRONG' WAY TO MASSAGE YOUR BABY. INFANT MASSAGE IS ABOUT BEING TOGETHER AND BEING IN TOUCH WITH EACH OTHER PHYSICALLY AND EMOTIONALLY.

❖

WHY MASSAGE?

❖

BABY MASSAGE IS SIMPLE TO LEARN and to do. It requires little extra 'equipment' and costs virtually nothing, except time. The long- and short-term benefits to infants are great, and massaging their children has a positive impact on parents, too.

BENEFITS FOR BABIES

❖ SECURITY
Positive physical contact between a parent and child makes the baby feel loved and valued. This feeling allows her self-esteem and self-confidence to develop.

❖ GENERAL WELL-BEING
Research shows that babies who are touched lovingly become ill and cry less often than those who are not. Massage can improve circulation and also boost the immune system, as it helps to move lymph fluid around the body, which clears harmful substances from the body. Massage may relieve pain and the symptoms of some ailments. It promotes relaxation and can help soothe a crying infant.

❖ PHYSICAL GROWTH
Massage promotes physical self-awareness, tones muscles and makes joints more flexible. In this way it is especially beneficial to premature babies (*see pages 62–65*), those with low birth-weight and children with special needs (*see pages 56–59*).

❖ SOCIAL SKILLS
Touching your baby teaches her about communication. Massage helps you establish a non-verbal communication with your child that enhances your early relationship with her, and therefore builds her self-esteem and sociability.

BENEFITS FOR PARENTS

❖ RELAXATION
When you massage your baby, you focus on her completely and interact with her. Parents report that they find this interaction enjoyable and relaxing.

❖ DEVELOPING SENSITIVITY
Because your baby cannot tell you if she likes a stroke or finds the pressure you apply uncomfortable, you must watch her reaction and interpret it. In this way, you learn to 'read' or understand her, which improves your parenting skills.

❖ CONFIDENCE BUILDING
Parents who are sensitive to their children tend to feel confident in their roles. Also, the physical contact of massage makes them comfortable with handling babies.

❖ PARENT-CHILD RELATIONSHIP
The non-verbal communication you share with your baby through massage sparks an interactive relationship with her that you can continue into the future. Massage can also become a regular time of intimacy between you.

RESEARCH EVIDENCE

A research study was carried out in Australia in 1992 with fathers and their babies to assess the impact of baby massage on the father-child relationship. A group of first-time fathers were shown how to massage their four-week-old babies, and asked to continue for the duration of the study. A control group of fathers who did not massage their babies was also monitored. It was found that at 12 weeks old, babies who were massaged greeted their fathers with more eye contact, smiling, vocalizing and touch than those in the control group. They showed more orientating responses to their fathers, and less avoidance behaviour. The fathers showed greater day-to-day involvement with their infants. Baby massage allows fathers and babies to enjoy the skin-to-skin contact that mothers often experience through breastfeeding, but fathers often miss out on. By massaging their babies, fathers come to understand their child's rhythms and responses, and become more confident about handling them.

PREPARING TO MASSAGE

❖

THE BEST TIME to massage your baby is when he is awake and feeling happy. You should be feeling calm and relaxed yourself, as your baby will pick up and be affected by your mood. Make sure you remove any jewellery and trim your nails to a suitable length, to avoid scratching his delicate skin. Gather everything you need around you, so that when you begin you can concentrate on the strokes, and on what your baby needs and likes, making the whole experience as soothing and pleasurable as possible for both of you.

USING OIL

WHY USE OIL?

Skin to skin contact promotes optimum growth and development, so undressing your baby and massaging him naked is a way of encouraging this. Oil helps your hands move over your baby's body smoothly, allowing you to make long, firm, continuous strokes without causing friction. Oil moisturizes skin, which can prevent or alleviate dryness.

WHICH OIL?

Use a natural oil, such as almond oil or grape-seed oil – these light, low-odour oils are easily absorbed by the skin and help to nurture it. Choose an organic variety if available. Natural oils are less likely than synthetic oils to irritate the skin. In countries where baby massage is a tradition, the oil used depends on availability. People from African and Asian cultures living in the West tend to use readily available oils that are similar to those used traditionally in their homelands, such as olive oil.

CAUTIONS

❖ Oiling your baby while massaging him may make him slippery, so beware of dropping him when you lift him up after you finish the massage. Pick him up in a towel until the oil has been absorbed by the skin.

❖ If you suspect that your child may be allergic to nuts or nut products, make sure you use an oil that you know to be free of nut products.

❖ Do not use essential oils (aromatherapy oils) on babies unless directed by a trained aromatherapist.

❖ Do not massage your baby if he has a temperature. This is particularly important if you are unsure of the cause.

❖ If your child has any form of cancer that is being treated actively, do not massage him, as you may spread the disease around the body. However, if your child is receiving palliative care, massage will be beneficial. Check with your doctor if you are unsure.

PATCH TEST

A patch test allows you to make sure your baby is not allergic to, or her skin irritated by, the oil you choose. Typical adverse reactions are a rash or a red inflamed area.

1 Place a little oil on the inside of your baby's wrist or ankle.

2 Leave for 20–30 minutes to allow time for a severe reaction to show. To eliminate sensitivity altogether, wait for 12–24 hours.

3 If there is no irritation after this time, proceed with the massage. If irritation does occur, DO NOT use the oil.

Lay your baby on a soft towel for the massage, so you avoid staining your clothes or carpet with oil, and can pick him up in the towel after the massage

WHAT YOU NEED FOR MASSAGE

❖ A WARM ROOM
Babies lose heat quickly when uncovered and oil tends to reduce body heat, so the room must be warm enough to keep your baby comfortable. 80ºF (26ºC) is the ideal room temperature. If you feel warm enough in short sleeves, the room is likely to be fine for massage.

❖ A SENSIBLE SCHEDULE
Massage your baby between feeds, when he is satisfied. If you massage him too soon after a feed you may induce vomiting – wait for at least an hour. If it is almost time for the next feed, he may become hungry and unsettled during the massage.

❖ TIME
Allow 20–30 minutes to perform a full-body massage to begin with. Rushing or trying to fit it in between other activities can be counterproductive as it may unsettle your baby. Once you are both familiar with the massage, you may need less time.

❖ A QUIET, CALM ATMOSPHERE
Both of you will enjoy the massage more if you are not distracted by noise from the television or radio, for example. You will 'tune in' to each other more effectively, so you can be responsive to your child and notice what he likes and dislikes.

Make sure you have a cushion to sit on to help keep your back straight

GETTING STARTED

❖

IF YOUR BABY has never been massaged, it may take her time to get used to it. Try it for three to four consecutive days initially, so you both become accustomed to the strokes. Once you feel confident and she seems comfortable with it, build it into your daily routine, or try to massage her at least three times a week. You can follow the routine in this chapter, but it is important to be guided by your baby's likes and dislikes. Use firm, reassuring strokes and make frequent eye contact with her throughout the massage.

WHEN, WHERE AND HOW TO MASSAGE

WHEN TO MASSAGE
Baby massage can be done at any time of the day. Many people like to massage babies after a bath, when the room is warm and the child is between feeds. Bathing relaxes the body and can act as a 'cue' that the massage is about to begin. In many cultures, massage is used to moisturize the skin, and so follows a bath naturally.

WHERE TO MASSAGE
Choose a warm, quiet room where you both feel comfortable. In hot climates, massage can take place out-of-doors, as long as the baby is in the shade. Lay your baby on a towel on a firm surface because this promotes good posture. The floor is a good place – you can sit down to massage and there is no edge for your baby to roll off.

PRESSURE OF STROKES
The pressure of your massage strokes should depend on the age of your baby. Strokes for newborns should be delicate – butterfly strokes are ideal (*see page 70*). Firm effleurage strokes (*see page 71*) can be used as the baby gets older or more confident. Firm strokes are also quite reassuring. If the skin reddens, reduce the pressure.

LEARNING TO RELAX

Babies absorb the tensions and anxieties of their parents, especially through physical contact. It pays for you to take time out for relaxation before beginning the massage in order for you and your baby to get the most from the experience. Clear your mind of thoughts of chores or other matters and allow yourself to give your full attention to the massage and your baby. The relaxation exercise shown here will help you unwind before you start to massage.

1 Clasp your fingers together and place your hands on your upper abdomen. Close your eyes and inhale deeply – you should feel your abdomen expand. Hold the breath for a few seconds, then exhale slowly.

2 Circle your shoulders backwards several times, then forwards. This helps relieve tension in the back, shoulders and neck. Shake your hands vigorously.

CHOOSING THE RIGHT POSITION

Make sure you are comfortable when you massage. Choose a position that allows you to keep your back straight, particularly while you are leaning forwards.

If you are massaging your baby on the floor, experiment with the three sitting positions shown here to find the one that suits you best.

KNEELING
Kneel on the floor with your knees resting on the towel, for extra comfort. Place a cushion on your calves, under your bottom, and sit back.

LEGS CROSSED
Sit on a cushion with your legs crossed. Place your baby directly in front of you. Lean forwards and give her a few massage strokes to check that this position is comfortable.

LEGS STRADDLED
Sit on a cushion with your legs outstretched on either side of your baby. You may need two cushions to keep your back straight, especially when reaching for the top of her body.

Try and keep your back straight when you lean forwards to massage

Relay positive messages about communication to your baby by giving her loving looks with tender strokes – you will both enjoy this

FRONT OF THE BABY

❖

ONCE YOU HAVE WARMED THE ROOM and have the oil and a towel ready, undress your baby and take off her nappy. Lay her down in front of you on her back, with her feet closest to you, ready to massage the front of her body. Dip your fingers in the oil, then rub your hands together to warm it. Each section of the massage begins with long, gliding strokes using the whole of the fingers and palms (effleurage strokes), which allow you to spread the oil and warm the muscles. These strokes also indicate to your baby which part of her body you are about to massage. Look into her eyes, smile and talk to her, then start the massage as shown below. Continue to talk to her during the massage to reassure her.

ARMS AND HANDS

1 EFFLEURAGE STROKES ACROSS THE CHEST Place your hands on the baby's abdomen, palms facing downwards and fingers pointing up the body – your fingertips should be level with the lower part of the chest. Glide both hands simultaneously up the chest towards the shoulders. Curl the fingers over the shoulders and stroke outwards to take hold of the upper arms. Move directly on to step 2.

2 STROKES ALONG THE ARMS Stroke down the arms and over the hands, then pull off at the fingertips. Make sure that both your hands are working simultaneously. Initially, your baby may not straighten her arms at the elbows. As her muscles relax, you can increase the gentle 'pulling' pressure of the stroke to straighten her arms. Perform steps 1 and 2 three or four times, or until the arms remain straight, even if momentarily.

3 WRINGING THE ARMS Circle your forefinger and thumb of each hand around your baby's right upper arm. On an older baby, place your hands side-by-side on her upper arm and wrap them around it. Twist your hands very gently in opposite directions in a wringing action. Use enough oil to allow your fingers or hands to slip around your baby's arm smoothly. Work down the arm in this way, pulling gently at the same time. Stop at the wrist and pull off at the hand with the forefinger and thumb of your left hand. Move on to the left arm. Repeat the stroke twice on each arm.

4 STRETCHING THE HANDS OPEN Support your baby's hand at the wrist with the palm facing upwards. Stroke the palm from the heel of the hand to the fingertips with the thumb of your free hand, then do the same with your other thumb. Do this once more, then repeat on the other hand.

ALTERNATIVE METHOD If you find it hard to open your baby's hands as shown left, hold her wrist with the palm facing downwards. Place your free thumb on the back of her hand near the wrist, and your fingers in her palm. Press your thumb and forefinger together, and move them towards the fingers.

5 PULLING THE FINGERS Hold your baby's wrist with the palm facing upwards, fingers towards you. Place your free forefinger and thumb on either side of the base of the finger. Pull along the finger to the tip, squeezing lightly. Pull each digit once, then repeat on the other hand.

THE CHEST

CIRCLES AROUND THE NIPPLES Place the first two
fingers of each hand in the centre of your baby's
chest, between the nipples. Move both sets of
fingers simultaneously, stroking upwards
and outwards, around the outsides of
the nipples and back to the centre.
Repeat several times.

*As you massage the chest,
increase and decrease the
size of the circles you make
around the nipples, so that
you touch as large an area
of the chest as possible*

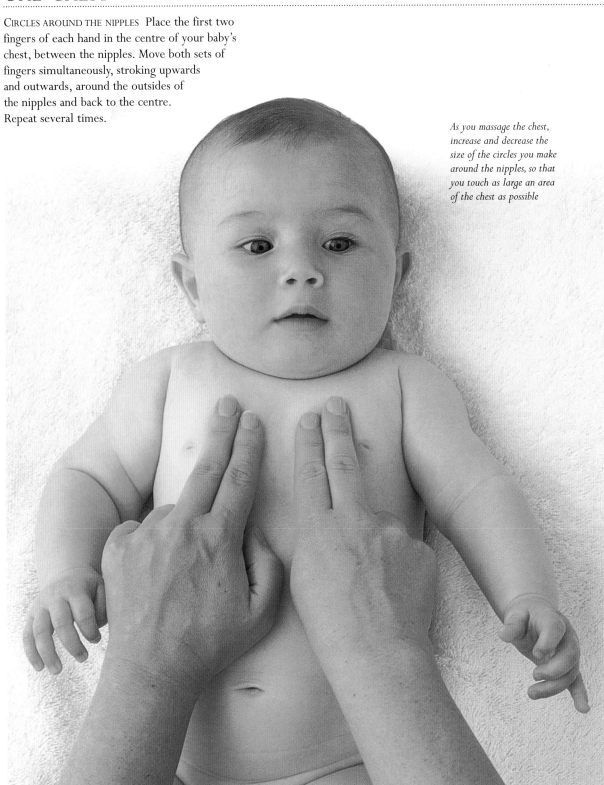

THE ABDOMEN

1 EFFLEURAGE STROKES DOWN THE ABDOMEN Place one hand horizontally across the abdomen, just below the chest, and stroke firmly down to the base of the abdomen, then lift off gently. Just before this hand loses contact with your baby's body, place the other hand across the top of the abdomen as before, and stroke down. Repeat several times, with one hand always in contact with your baby's body.

2 LITTLE CIRCLES AROUND THE NAVEL Place the first two fingers of one hand next to the navel. Press gently, making a circular movement. Release the pressure, slide your fingers around the navel slightly and repeat. Work in a clockwise direction, slowly spiralling outwards until you reach just inside the right hip.

3 LARGE CIRCLES AROUND THE ABDOMEN Starting just inside your baby's right hip, move the flat of your fingers upwards until they reach the right side of the rib cage, then across to the same point on the left side. Now stroke down to just inside the left hip and across the base of the abdomen back to the right hip. Repeat several times.

THE LEGS AND FEET

1 EFFLEURAGE STROKES ON THE UPPER
LEGS Hold your baby's ankle in
one hand. Place the other hand
horizontally across the top of her
thigh, with your fingers pointing
inwards. Rotate your wrist outwards
and fan your fingers across the thigh,
around to the back of the leg, so that
you are holding the thigh with your
thumb on top and fingers underneath.
Move directly on to step 2.

2 EFFLEURAGE STROKES ON THE
LOWER LEGS Massage down the
outside of the leg to the ankle. Keep
holding the ankle and place your free
hand back in the starting position,
with fingers pointing outwards. Rotate
your wrist inwards and stroke down,
massaging the inside of the leg in the
same way. Repeat steps 1 and 2 several
times on each leg.

3 ▶ WRINGING THE LEGS
Place both hands next
to each other on one of
your baby's thighs and wrap
them around it. Using light
pressure, twist your hands
very gently in opposite
directions in a wringing
action. Work down the leg,
pulling gently at the same
time. Stop at the ankle and
pull off at the feet using
your forefinger and thumb.
Repeat twice on each leg.

4 ▼ CIRCLES ON THE SOLES
Hold your baby's ankle
in one hand, with the knee
bent and the toes pointing
upwards. Place the thumb of
your free hand at the centre
of the sole, near the heel.
Press lightly, making a small,
circular motion. Repeat the
stroke up the centre of the
foot to the base of the toes.
Do this twice on each foot.

5 CIRCLES ON THE EDGES
OF THE FEET Continue
to hold your baby's foot in
one hand, knee bent, toes
pointing upwards. Place
your thumb on the sole
directly below the little toe,
and your forefinger at the
same position on the top
of the foot. Squeeze them
together, making a small,
circular movement at the
same time. Glide your
fingers a little way down
the edge of the foot and
repeat the stroke. Continue
in this way until you reach
the heel, then use the same
stroke to massage the other
edge of the same foot. Do
this twice on each foot.

6 STROKING THE ACHILLES' TENDON
Support your baby's calf in one hand, with the knee bent. Place your free forefinger and thumb on either side of the ankle bone. Stroke towards the heel, squeezing gently. Do this four times, then repeat on the other foot.

7 MASSAGING THE TOPS OF THE FEET
Hold the ankle with one hand, ensuring the knee is bent. Place the thumb of your other hand on the top of the foot near the ankle, and your forefinger under the foot. Squeeze slightly, hold the pressure, pull down over the foot and off at the toes.

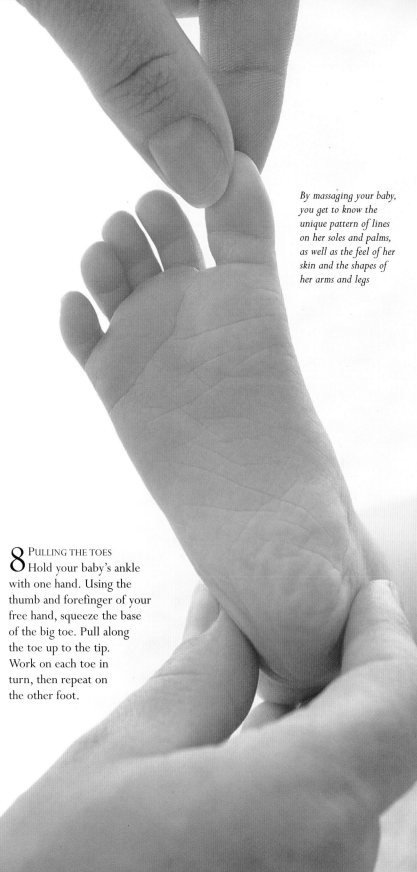

By massaging your baby, you get to know the unique pattern of lines on her soles and palms, as well as the feel of her skin and the shapes of her arms and legs

8 PULLING THE TOES
Hold your baby's ankle with one hand. Using the thumb and forefinger of your free hand, squeeze the base of the big toe. Pull along the toe up to the tip. Work on each toe in turn, then repeat on the other foot.

FINISHING STROKES ON THE FRONT

EFFLEURAGE STROKES ALONG THE BODY
Place your right hand on your baby's right
shoulder. Using your whole hand, stroke
diagonally across the chest and abdomen
to her left hip (*see below*). Continue to
stroke down the left leg to the ankle.
Do not let go of the ankle until you
have placed your left hand on your
baby's left shoulder. Now perform
the stroke on the opposite diagonal –
down to her right ankle. Repeat this
twice. Make sure your strokes are
firm, and that one hand is always
in contact with your baby.

*Baby massage provides an
opportunity for you and
your baby to engage in
'conversation' – with smiles,
talking and eye contact*

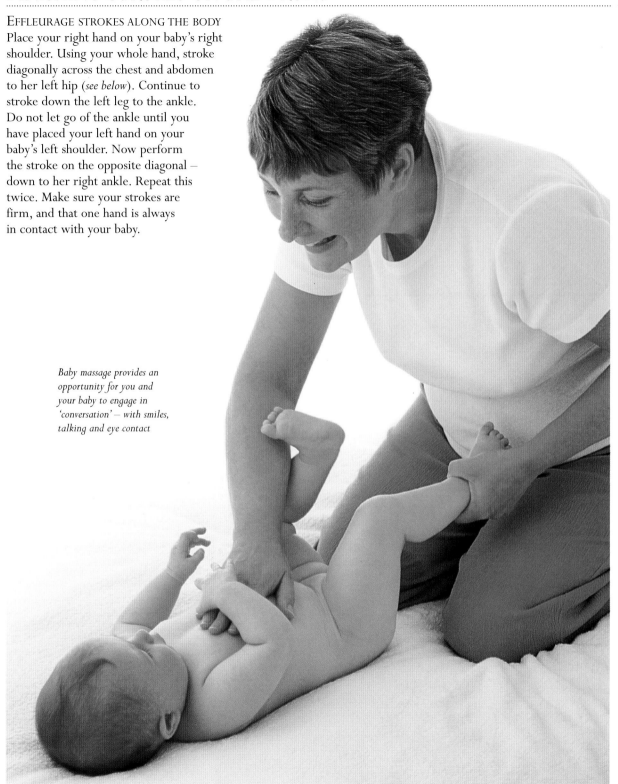

BACK OF THE BABY

❖

FOR THIS PART OF THE MASSAGE, position your baby on his tummy with his feet closest to you. If he is used to sleeping on his back or side, he may not like lying on his tummy, but try and encourage him to do so as it will contribute to his gross motor development. Massaging his back can be a pleasurable way of familiarizing him with this position. Initially, he may tolerate only a short stretch of time on his tummy, so perform as much of the back routine as he allows and build it up slowly. As he will not be able to see you, talk to him and make reassuring sounds to comfort him as you massage.

THE BACK

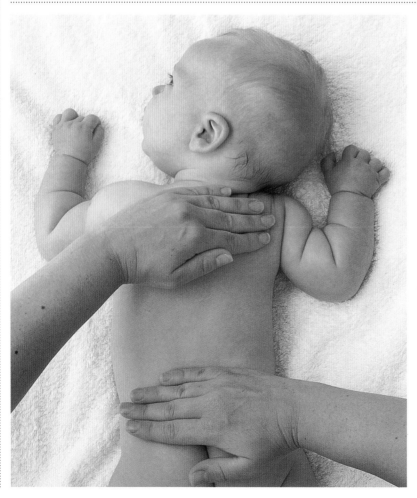

1 EFFLEURAGE STROKES DOWN THE BACK Place one hand horizontally across the top of your baby's back, just below his neck, and stroke firmly towards you. Lift your hand off when it reaches his bottom, but just before you do, place your other hand in the starting position. Stroke downwards as before. Repeat these strokes several times.

2 MASSAGING THE SHOULDERS Place one hand on either side of the neck and stroke along the shoulders towards the arms, using the whole surface of each hand. Repeat several times. Babies and parents often have identical tension spots, so if your own shoulders and neck tend to be tense, make a point of performing this stroke on your baby.

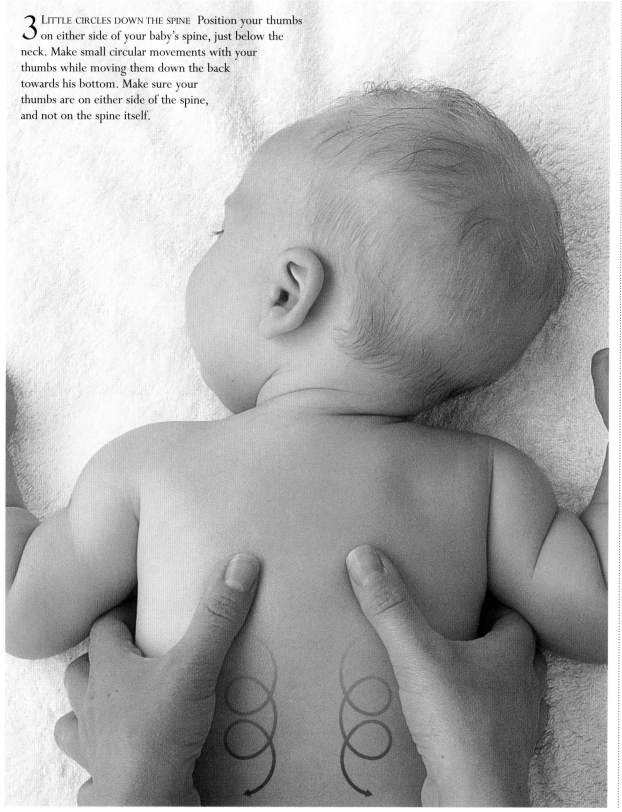

3 LITTLE CIRCLES DOWN THE SPINE Position your thumbs on either side of your baby's spine, just below the neck. Make small circular movements with your thumbs while moving them down the back towards his bottom. Make sure your thumbs are on either side of the spine, and not on the spine itself.

4 PULLING THE SIDES Place your hands horizontally across your baby's back (*see right*). Cross your arms and slide your right hand to his left side and your left hand to his right side. Bring your hands back to the starting position simultaneously, pulling the flesh on the sides of the torso gently towards the spine with your fingers. Make these horizontal movements several times, moving your hands up and down his back as you do so, so that you massage the sides along the whole length of the torso.

5 BIG STROKES ACROSS THE BACK AND SHOULDERS Place your hands next to each other on your baby's back, with your right hand closer to his head. Keeping your left hand in place, move your right hand to your baby's right side, then diagonally up towards and over the left shoulder. Then glide the hand down to his right hip. Now move your left hand towards his left side, then diagonally up and over his right shoulder (*see right*), and down to the left hip. Place your hands back in the starting position and repeat the stroke several times.

6 MASSAGING THE BASE OF THE SPINE
Place the heel of your hand in
the dimple directly above the centre
of your baby's bottom, at the base of
his spine. Circle clockwise with
gentle pressure several times.

THE BOTTOM

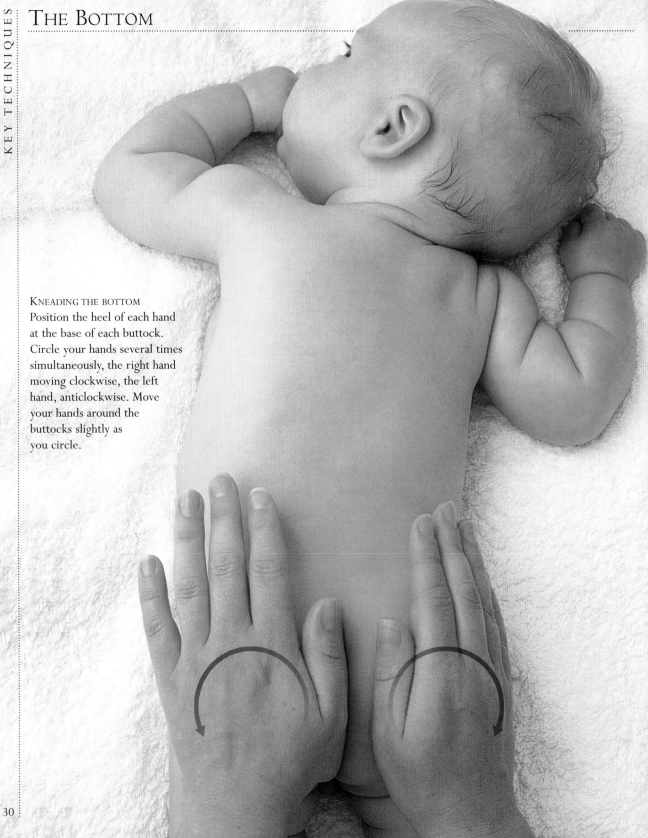

KNEADING THE BOTTOM
Position the heel of each hand
at the base of each buttock.
Circle your hands several times
simultaneously, the right hand
moving clockwise, the left
hand, anticlockwise. Move
your hands around the
buttocks slightly as
you circle.

THE LEGS

EFFLEURAGE STROKES DOWN THE LEGS Once you have finished kneading the bottom, move one hand down the leg towards the ankle in a firm, sweeping stroke. When you reach the ankle, begin the stroke on the other leg using your other hand. One hand should always stay in contact with your baby. Repeat several times.

FINISHING STROKES ON THE BACK

EFFLEURAGE STROKES DOWN THE BODY Place your left hand on your baby's right shoulder. Using the whole surface of your hand, stroke diagonally down the back, over the left buttock, and down the left leg to the foot. As you reach the foot, place your right hand on your baby's left shoulder (*see below*) and stroke diagonally down the body to the right foot. Repeat twice, using firm strokes, without losing contact with your baby's body.

HEAD & FACE

❖

INITIALLY, BABIES TEND TO RESIST head and face massage, particularly during the first few weeks of life, and especially if the delivery was long or traumatic. Try this part of the massage routine for three to four consecutive days, and if your baby seems unhappy with it or begins to cry, stop and massage other parts of his body, then try again in a few days or weeks. Once babies are accustomed to these strokes, they tend to enjoy them greatly, and even more so as they get older. For this part of the massage, lay your baby on his back with his feet closest to you. Make sure your strokes are light. Little or no oil is required.

THE HEAD

1 STROKING THE HEAD Cup your hands around your baby's head with your forefingers on his hairline. Moving your hands simultaneously, stroke backwards over the crown of the head until you reach the base of his skull. Move directly on to step 2.

2 STROKING THE JAW Part your hands and bring them to the sides of his face. Stroke along the jaw line with your fingers until they meet at the chin. Repeat steps 1 and 2 several times.

THE FACE

1 STRETCHING THE FOREHEAD Position your thumbs at the centre of your baby's forehead, just below the hairline. Stroke each thumb outwards in a straight line to the sides of the face. Repeat all the way down the forehead, as if you are drawing a series of lines with your thumbs.

2 MASSAGING THE TEMPLES On the last stroke across the forehead, place your thumbs in the centre, just above the eyebrows, and glide them across to your baby's temples gently, but firmly. Now make several small, circular strokes on the temples.

3 STROKING THE UPPER CHEEK BONES Place your thumbs on either side of the bridge of the nose. In a single flowing stroke, move each thumb simultaneously downwards and outwards, along the upper part of the cheek bone to the sides of the face.

4 STROKING THE LOWER CHEEK BONES Position your thumbs on either side of the bridge of the nose again, this time slightly lower down. Make a single sweeping stroke with each thumb from this position along the lower part of the cheek bone and out to the sides of the face.

5 CIRCLES ON THE TOP JAW LINE
Position your thumbs side-by-side on the dip above your baby's top lip. Pressing lightly, make small, circular movements with the thumbs. Glide each thumb outwards a little and repeat. Do this along the length of the top jaw line and out towards the ears.

6 CIRCLES ON THE LOWER JAW LINE
Place your thumbs side-by-side just below the centre of the lower lip. Using light pressure, make a circular movement with each thumb, then slide them outwards a little way and repeat. Do this along the lower jaw line, again, towards the ears.

7 ◀ SQUEEZING THE EARS Hold the outer edge of the upper ear between forefinger and thumb. From this position, make small circular strokes down the outer edge of the ear to the lobe.

8 ▼ SQUEEZING THE CHIN Starting at the centre of the chin, hold the flesh at the bottom of the chin between thumb and forefinger and squeeze gently. Repeat along the length of the lower jaw line to the ear, then on the other side of the chin. Alternatively, pinch both sides of the chin simultaneously using both hands.

9 STROKING THE HEAD Repeat the steps for the head massage on page 32 to finish the head and face massage.

STRETCHES

❖

ONCE YOU HAVE COMPLETED the main part of the massage – on the front, back, head and face – move on to the stretches. By now, your baby's muscles are warm and relaxed, so you can stretch the limbs and mobilize the joints safely. These stretches help to develop flexibility. For this part of the routine, lay your baby on her back with her feet towards you. Oil is not necessary. Most babies enjoy the stretches, especially when accompanied by playful noises, such as "weeeeeeee".

2 CROSSING THE ARMS Cross your baby's arms over her chest, crossing your own arms to do this. Hold the position for a few seconds. Repeat steps 1 and 2 several times. Each time you cross her arms, alternate which arm goes on top.

ARM STRETCHES

1 STRETCHING THE ARMS Hold the back of the wrists with your fingers and place your thumb in your baby's palms or on the inside of her wrists. Stretch her arms out to the sides, in line with the shoulders and at right angles to the body. Pull gently to straighten the arms. Hold for a few seconds, then move on to step 2.

LEG STRETCHES

CROSSING THE LEGS Take hold of your baby's ankles, one in each hand. Cross them over at the lower leg. Then grasp the point where they cross with one hand and move the knees up towards the abdomen, bringing the toes near the hips. In little 'bouncing' movements, press gently on the legs, easing them towards the abdomen. After a few bounces, cross the legs the other way and repeat.

3 ROTATING THE ARMS UPWARDS Stretch the arms out to the sides as for step 1. Keeping the upper arms (shoulder to elbow) in position, move the hands up towards the head, so that the arms bend at the elbows. The lower arms should be at right angles to the upper arms. Ensure the arms are resting on the towel.

4 ROTATING THE ARMS DOWNWARDS Without changing the position of the upper arms, raise the lower arms into the air so that the wrists are directly above the elbows, then bring them towards you down to the towel. The lower arms should be in line with the torso and the palms should rest on the towel. Repeat steps 3 and 4 several times.

37

ARM AND LEG STRETCH SEQUENCE

1 STRETCHING THE LIMBS Hold your baby's right wrist in your left hand, and her left ankle in your right hand. Pull both arm and leg away from the body gently at a slight angle, so the limbs form a diagonal line at each end of the torso. Hold the stretch for a few seconds, then move on to step 2.

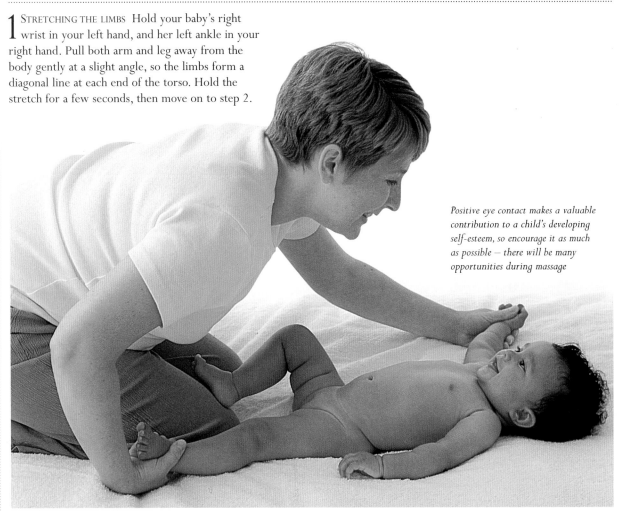

Positive eye contact makes a valuable contribution to a child's developing self-esteem, so encourage it as much as possible – there will be many opportunities during massage

2 FOLDING IN THE LIMBS – FOOT TO HIP Bring the left foot to the right hip (leading with the heel), and the right hand to the left hip, just above the thigh. Ensure the knee is bent. Hold for a few seconds, then move on to step 3.

3 STRETCHING THE LIMBS Repeat step 1, pulling your baby's right arm and left leg away from her body gently. Again, hold the position for a few seconds, then move directly on to step 4.

4 FOLDING IN THE LIMBS – FOOT TO SHOULDER Bring your baby's right arm straight down to the right hip, and take the left foot up to the right shoulder, again, leading with the heel. If your baby's foot does not reach the shoulder, do not force it, but take it as far as it will comfortably go. Repeat steps 1 to 4 with the same arm and leg, then twice with the alternate arm and leg.

FINISHING STROKES

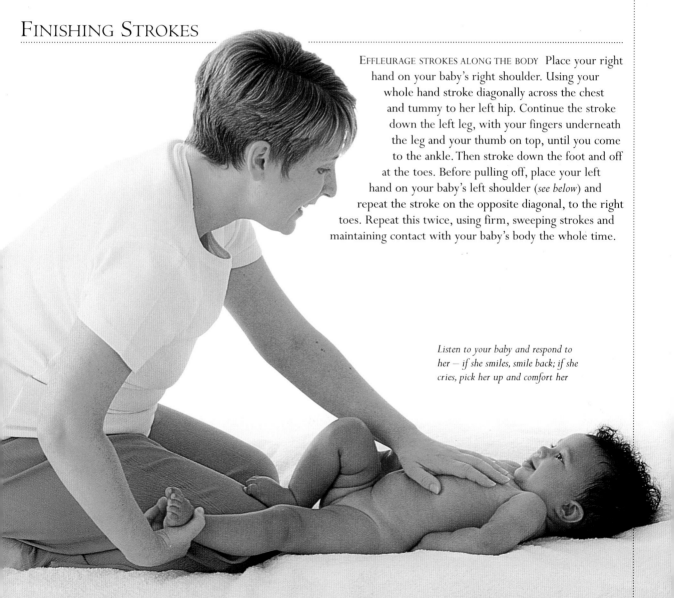

EFFLEURAGE STROKES ALONG THE BODY Place your right hand on your baby's right shoulder. Using your whole hand stroke diagonally across the chest and tummy to her left hip. Continue the stroke down the left leg, with your fingers underneath the leg and your thumb on top, until you come to the ankle. Then stroke down the foot and off at the toes. Before pulling off, place your left hand on your baby's left shoulder (*see below*) and repeat the stroke on the opposite diagonal, to the right toes. Repeat this twice, using firm, sweeping strokes and maintaining contact with your baby's body the whole time.

Listen to your baby and respond to her – if she smiles, smile back; if she cries, pick her up and comfort her

EVERYDAY CARE

❖

MASSAGE IS EASILY INCORPORATED INTO YOUR BABY'S DAILY ROUTINE. IN FACT, IT IS, AND HAS BEEN FOR CENTURIES, A VALUED PART OF EVERYDAY CHILD CARE IN MANY CULTURES, PARTICULARLY THOSE OF AFRICA AND ASIA — AND THE TECHNIQUES OF THESE TRADITIONS ARE VERY INSPIRING. THERE ARE MANY WAYS IN WHICH YOU CAN MAKE MASSAGE AND OTHER FORMS OF LOVING TOUCH A SPECIAL PART OF YOUR BABY OR TODDLER'S DAY-TO-DAY LIFE, AND IF YOUR CHILD HAS A SPECIAL NEED, REGULAR MASSAGE CAN BE PARTICULARLY BENEFICIAL.

❖

AFTER A BATH

❖

PARENTS OFTEN MASSAGE their babies after a bath, when the child is already naked. This is the best time to oil your baby if she has dry skin (*see page 87*), so carry out a full-body massage following the techniques on pages 18–39 once you have dried her. Even if her skin does not need moisturizing, you may find this the most natural time for massage. If you prefer to give her a full-body massage at a different time, just perform one or two of her favourite strokes, using the time between drying and clothing her to add more intimate moments to your daily routine.

SWADDLING
Your baby may find it comforting to be wrapped tightly in a towel after a bath, in a similar fashion to the Chinese custom of swaddling. You can begin to massage your baby at this point, through the towel. Make firm, long strokes down her arms (see left), then cup your free hand to stroke her head (see page 47). Holding your baby with her chest to yours, make long, sweeping strokes down her back with the whole of your hand.

USING EFFLEURAGE STROKES

Lay your baby on a dry towel in a warm room for massage. If performing only a few strokes, try effleurage strokes on her front, back, arms (*see page 18*) and legs (*see page 22*). These allow you to touch much of her body and can also be carried out on a sitting older baby. Use oil if you like, but this is not necessary.

STROKING THE FRONT OF THE BODY
Lay your baby on her back. Place your hand horizontally across the top of her chest and stroke downwards firmly until your hand reaches the base of her abdomen. Before your hand lifts off, place your other hand in the starting position. Stroke down as before. Repeat several times, making your strokes rhythmical.

STROKES DOWN THE BACK OF THE BODY
If your baby will lie on her stomach, follow the instructions for Effleurage Strokes Down the Back (see page 26). If she wants to sit up, you might need to support her, as these firm strokes may push her trunk forwards. To do this, place one hand on her chest, and use your other hand to stroke rhythmically down her back.

NAPPY CHANGING

YOU CAN MASSAGE YOUR BABY once or twice during the day when you change his nappy. Once you have cleaned him, and before you put on his nappy, stroke his tummy, legs and feet, with or without oil. This is a good method of massaging him as he gets older and refuses to keep still for a full massage, but be prepared for the fact that he may not stay still for this either. Try the sequence for a few days, starting with just a few strokes on his tummy and legs, adding more if he tolerates them. If your baby kicks, turns over or protests in other ways, stop — there are other ways of giving him loving touch, communicating with him and responding to his needs (*see pages 72–73*).

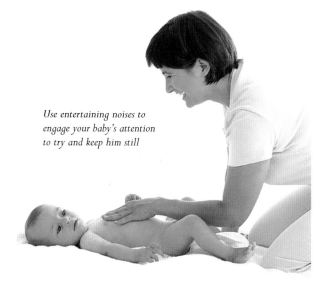

Use entertaining noises to engage your baby's attention to try and keep him still

TUMMY MASSAGE
Place your palm on your baby's abdomen. Using gentle pressure, make circular strokes in a clockwise direction with your palm, allowing your fingers to brush over his chest. Repeat several times, or for as long as your baby continues to enjoy it.

When your baby smiles at you, smile back — he will notice and enjoy it

RESEARCH EVIDENCE

The results of studies carried out in 1977 show that positive touch given in addition to routine handling during daily care (such as feeding and nappy changing) helps to develop child growth, language and social skills. In our practice we have found that this positive touch encourages children to feel loved and secure.

FOOT MASSAGE

Hold your baby's ankle in one hand and ensure his knee is bent. Use your free hand to hold the foot with your fingers on top and thumb underneath. Stroke firmly along the foot and pull off at the toes. Repeat several times on each foot.

LEG MASSAGE

Hold your baby's ankle in one hand. Place your free hand at the top of his thigh. Grasp the thigh, with your thumb on top and your fingers pointing upwards. Stroke down his leg to his ankle. Hold the ankle with this hand and grasp the other side of his thigh in the same way as before, this time with your other hand. Stroke down the leg to massage this side of his thigh. Repeat several times on each leg.

SOOTHING TO SLEEP

❖

MANY PARENTS instinctively use massage to soothe their babies into sleep. A routine can be developed before bed- or nap-time that acts as a cue for sleep. Once your baby is in her nightwear, lie her down in her cot, or cuddle her, and use strokes you know she finds particularly relaxing. Use the same sequence of strokes each time, keeping the routine short and simple. Make sure you stop before she actually falls asleep.

STROKING THE TUMMY
If your baby is lying on her back, she may enjoy a gentle tummy massage. Place your hand, palm downwards, on her abdomen. Move your hand in circles in a clockwise direction, stroking her with your fingers and the entire surface of your palm. Keep the pressure very light, reducing it gently as she becomes more relaxed and sleepy, until you are hardly touching her at all.

STROKING THE HEAD AND FACE

If you are holding and cuddling your baby while she falls asleep, massage her head and face gently. Using the back of one of your fingers, stroke her cheek slowly and rhythmically. Look at her and talk or sing to her quietly. To stroke her head, cup it in one of your hands, with your forefinger at her hairline. Now stroke backwards to the base of her neck. Do this gently, and for as long as she finds it soothing.

A CHILD PSYCHOLOGIST'S VIEW

SLEEPING ALONE Many infants fall asleep only when someone is with them. Cuddling is a vital part of parenting, but it is also important to your child's developing independence that she learns she can fall asleep alone. At about four months old, establish a sleep-time routine, such as tea, play, bath, bedroom, breast or bottle, and cot. Take her off the breast or bottle while she is still awake but drowsy. Put her into the cot, sit with her, possibly stroking her, until she falls asleep. Over a few weeks, reduce the 'help' you give, and begin to move out of the room, encouraging her to settle herself to sleep.

Sing softly to your baby when she is falling asleep

TODDLER PLAYTIME

❖

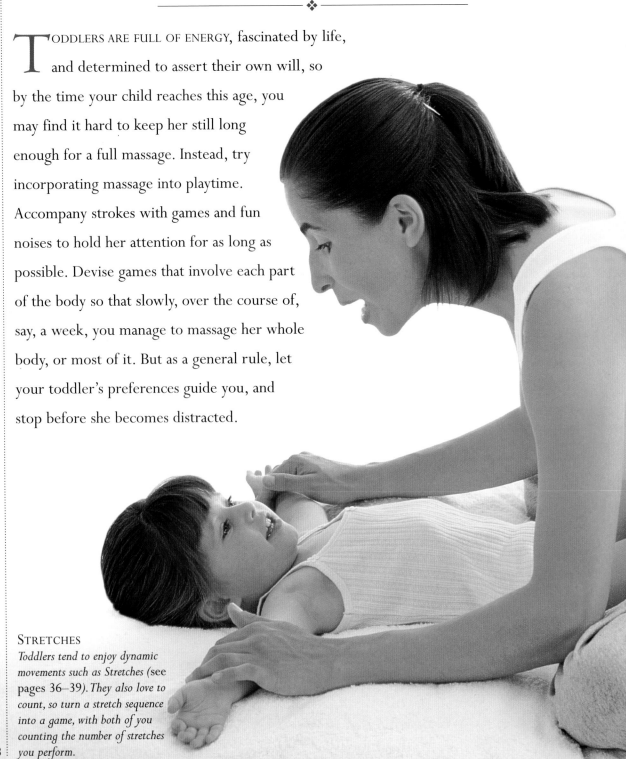

TODDLERS ARE FULL OF ENERGY, fascinated by life, and determined to assert their own will, so by the time your child reaches this age, you may find it hard to keep her still long enough for a full massage. Instead, try incorporating massage into playtime. Accompany strokes with games and fun noises to hold her attention for as long as possible. Devise games that involve each part of the body so that slowly, over the course of, say, a week, you manage to massage her whole body, or most of it. But as a general rule, let your toddler's preferences guide you, and stop before she becomes distracted.

STRETCHES
Toddlers tend to enjoy dynamic movements such as Stretches (see pages 36–39). They also love to count, so turn a stretch sequence into a game, with both of you counting the number of stretches you perform.

A CHILD PSYCHOLOGIST'S VIEW

ENCOURAGING SELF-CONFIDENCE Your child receives an important message when you massage her lovingly and play games with her: that you are interested in her and want to know how she feels. Assuring her in this way helps her maintain a secure attachment to you, which in turn encourages the development of her self-confidence.

Adapt how you position your child for massage as she grows taller – if massaging her head, face, arms or chest, bring her legs on to your lap so you can reach these areas

PLAYING WITH THE LEGS AND FEET
Try to adapt the strokes shown for the legs and feet (see pages 22–25) into a game such as 'climbing up the legs' or 'This Little Piggy'. By incorporating a little suspense into the game, you may hold her attention for that little bit longer. Make sure that your toddler's legs are supported and her knees are bent.

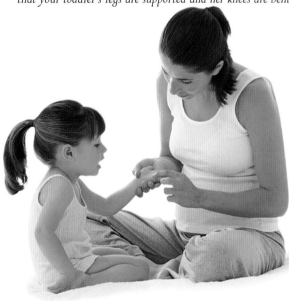

PLAYING WITH THE HANDS
Hold your child's wrist with one hand and use the thumb of your free hand to circle the palm, then pull down each of her fingers and stroke along them in turn with your forefinger and thumb. You could turn this into a game such as 'Round and Round the Garden'.

49

"*Massage* is something you and your baby do **together** — *it's about* **sharing feelings**, *and even* **thoughts**, *on an* **intimate**, *unspoken level* "

INDIAN MASSAGE

❖

IN MANY ASIAN CULTURES, particularly on the Indian sub-continent, baby massage is a traditional part of day-to-day care. Mothers learn the techniques from their own mothers or mothers-in-law. Sometimes, massage begins on the first day of life, but it usually starts when the baby is about five days old, once the umbilical cord stump has fallen off, and continues until the child can walk. Traditionally the oils used are mustard-seed oil in the winter, because it is warming, and coconut oil in the summer because of its cooling properties. There is often no set routine. Mothers start on the areas their baby likes best and work towards what is least enjoyed. Massage strokes and stretches are very like those shown in Key Techniques (*see pages 18–39*), and they have similar benefits.

An Indian mother or grandmother sits on the floor to massage her baby, with her legs outstretched and the baby on her lap

POSITIONS FOR INDIAN MASSAGE

If you would like to try massaging your baby while sitting in the Indian massage positions, ensure you keep your back straight – support your back against a wall if you need to. Once you are comfortable, place your baby on your lap in either of the positions shown here. Begin with the one that allows you to perform your baby's favourite strokes, then move on to the other.

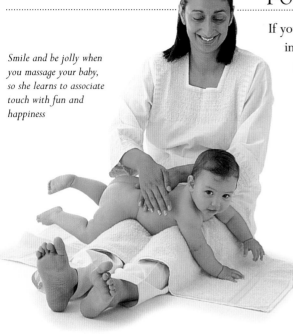

Smile and be jolly when you massage your baby, so she learns to associate touch with fun and happiness

ACROSS THE LAP

Use the techniques given for Back of the Baby (see pages 26–31), performing them with your baby lying across your lap. Once she has learned to turn over, she may not want to spend as much time on her back, so this position may be preferable.

ALONG THE LAP

With your baby in this position, you can easily massage her arms, hands, chest, abdomen and legs (see pages 18–24). You can also perform Stretches (see pages 36–39), but you may need to bring her slightly closer to you in order to massage her head and face (see pages 32–35).

AFRICAN MASSAGE

❖

DAILY CHILD CARE in many parts of Africa includes baby massage. Techniques differ from one African culture to the next, as do the oils used. Nigerian mothers use kernel or palm oil, whereas in Ghana, shea butter is preferred. Massage, which traditionally takes place after a bath, begins at birth and continues until the child is aged three or four. To begin with, it is carried out daily, but as a child grows older, he is massaged less often, perhaps three or four times a week. The techniques used can be vigorous, as it is felt that strenuous movements develop strength and flexibility.

HOT PRESSES

In some parts of Africa, a baby is wrapped in a towel and placed on his mother's lap after a bath. She applies a 'hot press' (simply a warmed flannel) all over his body, in order to relax the muscles in preparation for massage. During the first few months, these are also pressed on to the head in the belief that the skull can be teased into an attractive shape.

NIGERIAN BABY MASSAGE

Nigerians massage their babies to help them relax, sleep well and to moisturize the skin. The mother sits in a chair with the baby on her lap. She begins with long, firm, rhythmic strokes over the arms, abdomen, legs, feet and back. The head and face are then oiled with massage strokes. Stretches come next (*see below*), which are believed to develop strength, flexibility and muscle tone. These are followed by the most strenuous part of the routine, dangling. The baby is held up by one arm at a time (which is believed to strengthen his arms), before being held upside-down momentarily by the ankles. Finally, he is thrown into the air and caught several times, in the belief that this develops alertness.

CAUTION

Traditionally, babies are dangled by one arm, with no support. This technique, and the confidence to perform it safely, are handed down from mother to daughter. Without the guidance of an experienced demonstrator, use the adapted method shown here.

DANGLING

Sit on a chair with your baby on your lap. Place one hand under his bottom to support his weight, and hold his wrist firmly in your other hand. Stand up slowly, taking his weight in your supporting hand. Lift his arm and bring your supporting hand down fractionally – his raised arm will stretch. Pull it upwards gently for a few seconds, then take his weight fully in your supporting hand again. Repeat with his other arm. Always take the majority of his weight in your supporting hand, and watch his reaction to ensure he is comfortable.

STRETCHES

1 Lie your baby face-down across your lap. Take the arm furthest from your body behind his back and pull it very gently towards the centre of his back, holding it straight at the elbow (*see right*). Stroke firmly from the shoulder to the wrist and pull off at the fingers.

2 Take the leg furthest from you and bend it at the knee, bringing the heel to the buttocks. Repeat several times, then stroke firmly down the legs. Change your baby's position so he faces the opposite direction and repeat on his other arm and leg.

55

CHILDREN WITH SPECIAL NEEDS

❖

CHILDREN WITH DOWN'S SYNDROME or Cerebral Palsy often have low muscle tone, which massage can help to develop. It can also increase body-awareness; this is useful to visually impaired children, too. If your child has a special need, talk to her physiotherapist or doctor about how to massage her. Remember that she has her own rhythms that deserve respect.

MASSAGE FOR SPECIAL NEEDS

BENEFITS OF MASSAGE

Massage can:
❖ increase a child's body-awareness
❖ boost muscle tone
❖ encourage non-verbal communication to develop between parent and child
❖ help with bonding and attachment
❖ soothe and calm children and help parents to relax
❖ allow parents to feel they are helping their child positively.

PRESSURE OF STROKES

Children with special needs often have a sensory difficulty, in that they can be either highly sensitive or insensitive to touch. They need either light or deep pressure, depending on their 'sensory integration'. Some children actually dislike light touch, so firm pressure is needed. If you are unsure about the pressure of your strokes, watch your baby's reaction and ask your doctor or physiotherapist for advice.

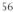

CHILDREN WITH DOWN'S SYNDROME

If your child has Down's Syndrome, his muscle tone may be low. Regular full-body massages, incorporating Stretches (*see pages 18–39*), help to increase muscle tone. Alternatively, he may have high muscle tone; in this case, massage can relax his muscles. If he has physiotherapy, perform a quick massage before the sessions – warming the muscles before physiotherapy may enhance the work done during a session.

Some children with Down's Syndrome may experience hearing impairments, which massage can also help with (*see below*). In order for children with this condition to make the most of their talents and abilities, they need plenty of stimulation to respond to. Massage can be another form of stimulation that you provide for your child. It is likely that he will enjoy the massage greatly – children with Down's Syndrome tend to be sociable, and their cheerful and affectionate characters respond well to affectionate touch. Massage has best results when it is something the two of you do together – a kind of touch-communication – rather than something you do to your child. Perhaps if your child has a sibling, you can encourage them to massage each other, allowing the whole family to share this form of communication. This can help improve your family relationships and make your child very happy.

CASE HISTORY

"Jack loves being massaged. When he was nearly two, a friend who had been to baby-massage classes with her baby suggested I massage Jack. She showed me some of the strokes she had learned. I tried them out on Jack, and his pleasure was so obvious that I wanted to learn more. Once I had the OK from my doctor, I went to a local clinic where they teach baby massage, and picked up a few more strokes. Now we do these every day. We have developed our own routine, starting with the strokes Jack likes most, but this is flexible, because Jack sometimes likes to decide which stroke comes next, telling me which one by performing it on me. He likes to massage me as well, and also massages his father and older sister frequently."

CHILDREN WITH SENSORY IMPAIRMENTS

Massage helps children who are visually impaired build a picture of the world around them, because being touched teaches them to touch, and touch helps them to explore their surroundings. A visually impaired child's body-awareness also increases through massage – she learns how long her arms and legs are, and gains a better idea of their shape. Massage can open new pathways of communication between you and your child, which will be a major source of comfort and security for her. Touch-stimulation increases the levels of responsiveness of children with sensory impairments, so massage can teach her to engage in social interaction. When you massage your child, make sure you always keep one hand on her body if she has impaired vision, and talk to her to reassure her. If your child has difficulty hearing, talk to her throughout the massage to stimulate her hearing. Tell her what you are doing, to help her link words and sounds to actions.

CASE HISTORY

"Our doctor suggested I try baby massage to help Isaac become more aware of touch, sounds and smells. I don't think he knew how to respond to it at first, but now he knows what it is and likes it very much. In fact, I think he looks forward to it. He started reaching out towards sounds, wanting to touch what he was hearing. Although he began crawling later than most 'normal' babies, it was not that much later. Other mothers of partially-sighted babies that I know have been inspired by how he's getting on, and now also use massage."

CHILDREN WITH CEREBRAL PALSY

Massage allows children with Cerebral Palsy to experience movements they cannot make alone, and increases their body-awareness. Each child's requirements are unique, so speak to your child's physiotherapist to establish how massage can enhance the work done in the sessions. Regular massage enables your child to benefit frequently from movements that stimulate her physical development. Here, we show part of the routine Cordelia and her mother share before a physiotherapy session.

MASSAGING THE FOOT
By massaging the soles of Cordy's feet gently with the pads of her fingertips, Cordy's mother stimulates the muscles along the leg, which react by tightening. This slowly strengthens them.

BENDING AND FLEXING THE LEG
With the heel supported in one hand, and the knee held in the other, Cordy's mother bends and flexes Cordy's leg gently to familiarize her with this 'walking' movement.

STRETCHING AND SITTING

1 STRETCHING THE ARMS UP Cordy lies on her back with her feet on her mother's lap. Cordy's mother holds her wrists gently and stretches her arms above her head.

2 STRETCHING THE ARMS DOWN Now Cordy's mother brings Cordy's arms down to her sides. She repeats steps 1 and 2 several times. These movements stimulate the muscles in the upper arms and along the shoulders.

3 SITTING UP Cordy's mother helps Cordy come to a sitting position by pulling her arms gently. This stimulates muscles in Cordy's arms, back and abdomen, and also in her legs, which push against her mother's lap to maintain balance as she rises up.

CASE HISTORY

"Cordy cried for weeks after the birth. Her condition was not detected immediately, so the crying was attributed to all sorts of things. When it was discovered that she had Cerebral Palsy, we were devastated. Her condition became noticeable when she began to move her arms and legs more, as we found she used one side of her body more than the other. Initially, she disliked physiotherapy, probably because she found it difficult, and could not understand what was happening to her. I think it put her off being touched. The physiotherapist said she might relax more if we helped her do some of the movements they did together at home. We turned many of these into a game. She liked those! It did help her to relax, and now she likes to be touched."

MASSAGE FOR DIFFERENT AGE GROUPS

❖

As your child develops, so do his needs, and whether he is a premature baby or a boisterous toddler, massage increases your sensitivity to him, enabling you to recognize his requirements, and decide how best to alter your approaches in response. Adapting your massage techniques, routines and the pressure of your strokes to suit your child's changing physical and emotional needs encourages your child in each stage of development and gives him the sense that you are moving with him through his experience of life.

❖

PREMATURE BABIES

❖

PREMATURE BABIES in neonatal units are handled frequently as part of the essential medical and nursing care they need. They often find this type of touch disturbing and distressing. Stroking or massaging them acts as a pleasing contrast, and provides them with comfort and love. Research has shown that when premature babies receive routine care in hospital, their pulse rates increase and their oxygen levels decrease, indicating distress. When they are massaged, however, the opposite occurs: their pulse rates come down and their oxygen levels rise, suggesting that they find massage calming and soothing.

CHOOSING A TIME AND PLACE

WHEN TO MASSAGE

Stroke or massage your baby after his routine care. This will help to calm and relax him, and he may also be more awake and alert at this time. You can massage him for up to 15 minutes, depending on his condition, and how much he can tolerate. If you want to touch and stroke your baby when he is asleep, you can do so provided he is not disturbed or over-stimulated by it. Before massaging your baby, talk to the nursing and medical staff about what you intend to do.

MASSAGE IN AN INCUBATOR

If your baby is being ventilated or is too sick to move, you can massage him very gently through the portholes of his incubator. Using the tip of your forefinger, make a few tiny strokes on his hand or face. If he has no adverse reaction, carry on. Once you are confident, stroke his back, arms, legs and head, using two or more fingers very lightly. These initial strokes introduce him to touch.

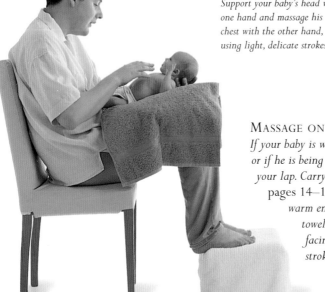

Support your baby's head with one hand and massage his chest with the other hand, using light, delicate strokes

MASSAGE ON YOUR LAP

If your baby is well enough to be taken out of the incubator, or if he is being nursed in a cot, you can massage him on your lap. Carry out the right preparations for massage (see pages 14–15), ensuring in particular that the room is warm enough. Then sit on a comfortable chair with a towel across your lap. Place your baby on his back facing you and begin the massage, using the strokes shown on pages 64–65.

BENEFITS OF MASSAGE FOR PREMATURE INFANTS

Perhaps the most important benefit of massaging your premature baby is that it helps you and your child to bond, which is especially important if he has spent the first days of his life in an incubator. It also gives you the knowledge that you are doing something positive for your baby. Massage can also:

❖ improve weight gain

❖ enhance growth and development

❖ encourage greater responsiveness

❖ improve digestion and metabolism

❖ reduce pain – massage stimulates the production of endorphins, the body's natural pain killers.

If your baby does not respond positively to massage, there are other ways of bonding – cuddles, soft words and gentle strokes all bring you closer together

MASSAGE STROKES

Premature babies should initially be massaged with a
very light touch. The pressure of the stroke should be as
light as you would use to stroke your closed eyelid with
your forefinger. Use butterfly strokes (*see below*) in the
early days or weeks, and once your child is accustomed
to these, start using the squeezing technique (*see right*).
After a while, when you feel your baby is ready,
introduce firm, long (effleurage) strokes (*see opposite*).

GENTLE SQUEEZING
*Squeezing can be performed on the arms and legs. Always ensure
that the elbow or knee is bent, and that the wrist or ankle is
held in your free hand to support the limb. Starting at the top
of the limb, squeeze the flesh on the outside of the arm or leg
very gently between your fingers and thumb, working down
towards the hand or foot, then repeat on the opposite limb.*

BUTTERFLY STROKES
*Using the very tips of your fingers, stroke lightly over your
baby's head, then down his chest, abdomen, arms and legs.
Make your strokes slow and rhythmical, using alternate hands.*

*As you finish a stroke, begin a new
one so that one hand is always in
contact with your baby's body*

EFFLEURAGE STROKES

As your baby grows accustomed to massage, you can replace the fingertip touch with longer, firmer strokes, using the whole of your hands. This enables you to have more physical contact with your baby. You can use these strokes to massage the front and back of your baby's body (see pages 21 and 26), and his arms (see pages 18–19). To massage his legs, support your baby's leg at the ankle with one of your hands. Using your other hand, fingers together, stroke gently but firmly down his leg.

CASE HISTORY

"Ellis and Spencer were born five weeks premature – not unusual for twins. They spent the first week of their lives in an incubator, with tubes all over their tiny bodies. This was very frustrating for me and my husband, as physical contact with them was so limited. All we wanted was to take them home, but we could barely touch them.

I used to put my hands through the portholes of their incubators and stroke them gently. If either of the twins was at all grisly, I would stroke his head and eyebrows, and it would calm him. If I made my strokes lighter and lighter, he would eventually nod off.

I started to stroke their tummies and tickle them behind their ears, which would often make them attentive. Even now, when feeding either of them, if his concentration wonders, I tickle him under the chin, which seems to focus his attention on the feed.

Having that initial contact with the twins, when they were in their incubators, allowed both me and my husband to bond with them. They still seem to enjoy massage at 10 weeks – it's part of their bedtime routine. They also find our voices quite calming, and they like to lie on my chest and hear my heartbeat – I think they find it very comforting."

WHEN NOT TO MASSAGE

Baby massage can be used to soothe and relax most premature infants. However, when you are stroking or massaging your baby, it is important that you watch his reactions, especially if he is in an incubator. You should stop the massage immediately if your baby's colour changes, he starts to cry or vomit, his breathing becomes more rapid, his pulse rate increases, or if his muscles become tense. If any of these changes occur, inform the medical or nursing staff straight away, or contact your doctor.

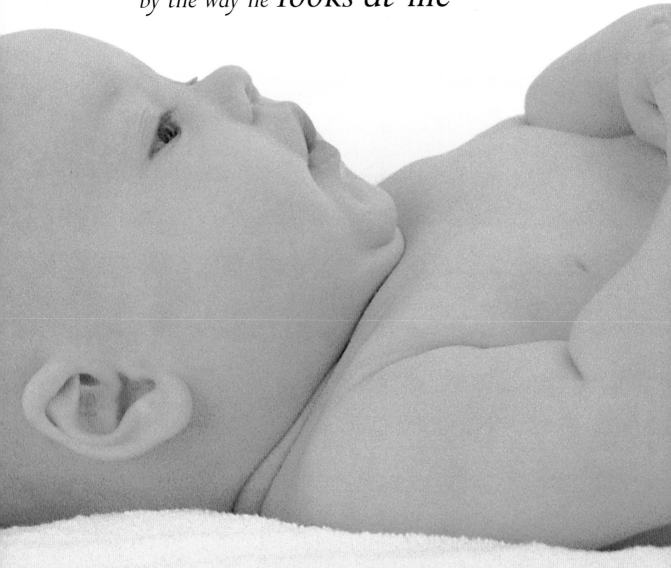

" *The* eye contact *between us is incredible,*
sometimes I feel *I know exactly*
what is going through his mind,
by the way he looks at me "

NEWBORN BABIES

MASSAGING YOUR NEWBORN BABY is a lovely way to get to know her – her expressions and reactions to different strokes, the contours of her body, the feel of her tiny fingers and toes. You will find that these special moments of loving touch are times that your baby comes to anticipate and enjoy. Massaging can also help her progress to the 'quiet, alert state' where she becomes calm, receptive,

If your newborn allows you to massage her head, take special care over the fontanelle

and seeks eye contact with you, which will create a wonderful feeling of intimacy between you. She may not smile, but you will have a sense of real closeness. This social interaction enhances your early relationship, setting strong foundations for the future.

Introducing Massage

When to Start

Baby massage can start on the day your baby is born, as happens in some cultures where infant massage is a tradition. If you feel confident and ready to begin during the first few days after the birth, then do so. Make sure you avoid touching the navel area until the umbilical cord stump has fallen off. This usually happens four to seven days after delivery.

Clothing and Seating

Some parents may initially prefer not to undress their babies for massage until both parent and child become accustomed to it. In this case, the baby can be dressed in a vest or babygro. Newborn babies, like older babies, can be massaged on the floor, but, to start with, you may find your baby prefers the

comfort and security of your lap. You can either sit on a comfortable chair, or on the floor. Place a towel over your lap to make your baby more cosy. If you choose the floor, try leaning against a wall to help you keep your back straight.

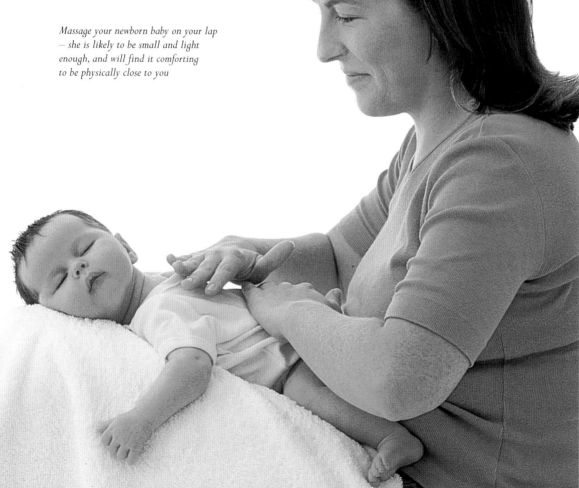

Massage your newborn baby on your lap — she is likely to be small and light enough, and will find it comforting to be physically close to you

BUILDING UP A ROUTINE

Baby massage is most beneficial for your baby when it forms part of her daily routine of care. Do not worry if you find it difficult to fit it in every day. Massaging your baby as little as three times a week will still have positive results. When you introduce the massage routine, start with just a few strokes, slowly building up to a full massage over the course of three to four weeks. Begin with a short five-minute session, using butterfly strokes (*see below*). Then introduce long, gliding (effleurage) strokes (*see right*), using more pressure. As you both gain confidence, you can remove your baby's clothes and massage her using oil. Gradually add more strokes until the routine has developed into a 15–20 minute full-body massage (*see pages 18–35*), ending with Stretches (*see pages 36–39*).

INCORPORATING STROKES

There are two ways of adding new strokes to your routine:

❖ Massage each part of the body – the front, back, head and face – incorporating more strokes into each section every time until you are using all the key techniques.

❖ Start on the front of the body (*see page 18*), move on to the back (*see page 26*), the head and face (*see page 32*), then add Stretches.

BUTTERFLY STROKES

Babies find delicate butterfly strokes soothing and pleasing. They are the best strokes to use to familiarize your newborn baby with massage and touch. Use both hands in succession, making slow, light and rhythmical strokes with the tips of your fingers, over your baby's head and face, chest, abdomen, limbs and back.

EFFLEURAGE STROKES

When you and your baby are comfortable with butterfly strokes, progress to the bigger, firmer strokes known as effleurage strokes. Babies find these reassuring, and they enable you to touch a larger proportion of your baby's skin than fingertip-touching allows. Stroke with the whole of your palms and the flat of your fingers over your baby's abdomen (see page 21), arms (see page 18), legs (see page 22) and back (see page 26), with one hand always touching your baby.

If you sit on the floor, raise your knees to reach your baby more easily

IF YOUR BABY DISLIKES IT

Some babies enjoy massage straight away, while others take three to four days to get used to each stroke. Massaging on consecutive days will help. Often newborn babies dislike having their head or neck touched for a few weeks, particularly if the birth was long or traumatic, or if the umbilical cord was caught around the neck. If your baby seems unhappy or cries during massage, try another stroke. If she is still unhappy, stop, wrap her in a towel, pick her up and give her a reassuring cuddle. Resume the massage once she has relaxed, or try again the next day.

A CHILD PSYCHOLOGIST'S VIEW

DANCE OF COMMUNICATION Babies have a strong motivation to connect with people. Even when your baby is very young, she will react to your voice and your touch, so use them to communicate your feelings for her.

As she begins to recognize the things you do, she will respond to them in her own way. And as you learn to recognize her responses, and respond back, the two of you establish a 'dance of communication', long before your baby uses language.

This 'dance' may start with the two of you gazing at each other, then move on to smiling at each other. Slowly, your baby will begin to imitate your expressions, until

eventually, her communications become vocal and you begin to hear emerging words.

To encourage your baby's developing communication skills, keep the 'dance' alive. Give her sounds, words, expressions and caresses to respond to, and continue to return her responses. You will enjoy these 'conversations' as much as your baby does, especially as her progress becomes evident.

By paying such close attention to her, you will also learn to recognize your baby's rhythms – when she likes to be calm and quiet and when she wants to be stimulated. You can then respond to her appropriately.

OLDER BABIES

❖

ONCE YOUR BABY IS ROLLING OVER, sitting up or crawling, you will find it hard to give him a full-body massage, as he will rarely lie still. Go with this. If you still want to massage him, you must be flexible. If he rolls over from his back on to his front, for instance, massage his back. This wriggling may continue until your child is two or three years old.

MASSAGE, TOUCH AND COMMUNICATION

Some older babies are happy to be massaged while sitting up. With your baby in this position, you can massage his arms (*see pages 18–19*), his back (*see pages 26–28*), and perform arm stretches (*see below*) – many babies enjoy these. If he resists massage, do not persist: he is telling you he does not want it.

MASSAGE SITTING UP

1 Sit on the floor with your baby facing you. Stretch your baby's arms straight out to the sides. Pull the arms outwards gently and hold the position for a few seconds.

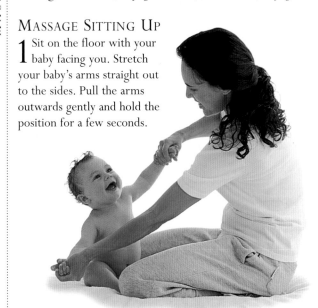

2 Cross your baby's arms over his chest, with his right arm over his left arm. Repeat step 1, then cross his arms again, this time with left arm over right. Repeat steps 1 and 2 several times.

PHYSICAL CLOSENESS

Although massage is a lovely way to be physical with your baby, it is important that you do not continue if he would rather not be massaged. You can find other ways of being close to him. Sing songs or rhymes that involve actions such as bouncing him on your knee. Or you can simply cuddle him on your lap.

SEPARATION ANXIETY

Around the time that massage becomes less possible, you may notice that your child begins to experience 'separation anxiety'. He may cry each time you leave the room and want to be carried for long periods of time. This happens because he wants to feel secure in exploring the world and is testing his security – you. If you give him the feeling of security he needs now, it will help him to become confident and independent in time. Pick him up and take him with you if you move across or out of the room. Do not see this as a tie or a chore, but as an opportunity to be close and to help him feel safe.

COMMUNICATING THAT YOU UNDERSTAND HIS NEEDS

As your baby becomes older, he will start initiating communication. He will try and indicate to you what he does and does not like, by refusing the breast or a spoonful of food, for example. Respond to his communications in a way that makes it clear that he is understood. If he shows he is not enjoying a massage stroke, try another that you know he likes. At this stage of his development, he needs to know that you can understand what he is trying to express, and can give him what he needs from you.

Your baby's needs will continue to develop – responding to them appropriately can be a challenge. During the first eight to nine months, he needs you to be consistent and reliable, so he knows you are there for him.

A CHILD PSYCHOLOGIST'S VIEW

RESPONDING TO HIS NEEDS If you respond consistently to your baby's requirements, he will know he can rely on you to understand and meet his needs. This has a positive impact on his emotional and psychological development. A sense of security during infancy is the foundation for a healthy emotional life.

Use physical touch to let your baby know that you understand his needs, particularly if he shows anxiety about being separated from you

TODDLERS

❖

WHEN YOUR CHILD STARTS TO WALK, a massage routine becomes impossible; it will be difficult to get him to sit still, let alone lie still. You can reintroduce massage when your toddler is two and a half to three years old, depending on his personality. Until then, communicate with him using other touch techniques. He will love cuddles on your lap and having his hair stroked. When you talk to him, touch his arm or leg gently. Stroke his tummy or back as part of his bedtime routine, together with kisses and cuddles. Play games and sing songs that involve touch, smiles and eye contact. You will enjoy giving him this attention as much as he loves to receive it, and he will know you love and value him.

GROWING INDEPENDENCE

ASSERTING HIS WILL

To test his growing independence, your toddler will frequently try to assert his will. Often, parents mistake this behaviour as willfulness in the adult sense, and feel they have somehow failed in their parenting. But this is not the case. It is a natural step in every child's development. However, toddlers often do not know what they want or what is best for them. That is why they need their parents to help them.

LETTING HIM CHOOSE

Even if he has enjoyed massage for many months, a toddler may suddenly decide "Not today". This is fine. You have to insist on some things — a warm coat on a cold day, for instance — but massage can wait. Your toddler may allow you to massage parts of his body: his back, face or arms, until you find he is enjoying the process he initially refused. But if he continues to refuse, be sensitive to his wishes.

Cuddles, games and eye contact are valuable ways of showing your toddler that you love him and enjoy being with him

ROUTINES AND BOUNDARIES

If your toddler lets you massage her and enjoys a certain stroke in particular, go ahead and repeat it. This shows her she can influence you, and that you notice what feels good to her. A little later in her development she may begin making demands for what she wants, using words such as "more" or "again".

This is a good time to establish boundaries. Your efforts to understand and respond to your baby's needs reap rewards at this stage, as you must be able to distinguish between what she needs and what she simply wants in order not to deny your child anything essential. When appropriate, say "No", but be prepared for her to test the boundaries. For example, she may try to extend her bedtime routine by asking for "one more story". This is when parents know best – one or two stories are enough! Keeping boundaries and routines is part of good parenting – do it gently and clearly.

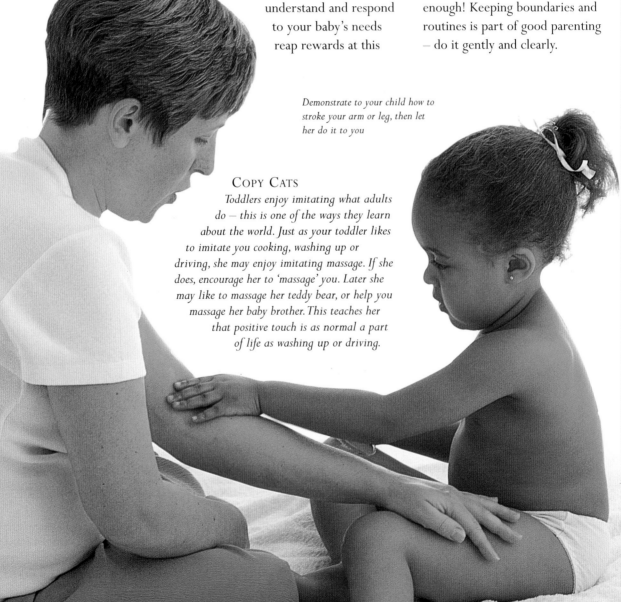

Demonstrate to your child how to stroke your arm or leg, then let her do it to you

COPY CATS

Toddlers enjoy imitating what adults do – this is one of the ways they learn about the world. Just as your toddler likes to imitate you cooking, washing up or driving, she may enjoy imitating massage. If she does, encourage her to 'massage' you. Later she may like to massage her teddy bear, or help you massage her baby brother. This teaches her that positive touch is as normal a part of life as washing up or driving.

EASING COMMON PROBLEMS

❖

IT IS UNLIKELY THAT YOUR CHILD WILL
PASS THROUGH INFANCY AND EARLY
CHILDHOOD WITHOUT ENCOUNTERING
SOME OF THE MINOR AILMENTS, OR OTHER
SOURCES OF DISTRESS, THAT ARE COMMON
TO THESE AGE GROUPS. BABY MASSAGE
CAN HELP TO EASE THE PAIN AND
DISCOMFORT CAUSED BY SOME OF THESE
PROBLEMS, BUT EVEN WHEN IT DOES NOT,
MANY PARENTS OFTEN FIND IT WORKS
WELL AS A COPING STRATEGY WHEN A
CHILD IS UNWELL. IT ALLOWS YOU TO FEEL
YOU HAVE TRIED YOUR BEST TO HELP.
BABIES SENSE THIS CONCERN, AND CAN
BE COMFORTED BY IT.

❖

COLIC & WIND

❖

COLIC CAN START when a baby is five days old and continue daily until he is 12 to 14 weeks old. The baby feels a severe abdominal pain that nothing seems to ease, causing him to cry for long periods of time. Commonly, the crying is worse during the evenings. Babies with wind experience similar pain and often cry until the wind is passed. After carrying a distressed and inconsolable baby around for hours, parents often feel helpless, exhausted and very distressed themselves. They may also feel disillusioned, as the reality of colic is far from the vision of parenthood they might have had. Certain massage strokes can help to relieve colic temporarily or expel wind. By bringing some relief to their baby, parents may also feel more able to cope with the ongoing situation.

COPING WITH COLIC AND WIND

SIGNS AND SYMPTOMS
Typically, babies with wind or colic:
❖ are difficult to wind
❖ become fretful when lying on their backs
❖ bring their knees up to their chests frequently
❖ are less distressed when held in an upright position
❖ arch backwards
❖ have a distressed cry that does not stop when they are picked up, or stops, then recommences.

THINGS TO TRY
As each baby is different, techniques that relieve one baby may not work for another. You could try:
❖ holding positions (see opposite)
❖ carrying your baby positioned over your shoulder
❖ movement – putting your baby in to a rocking baby seat or rocking him in your arms, walking him around in a sling, pushing him in a pram or taking him for a drive
❖ giving him a deep, warm, relaxing bath; take him in the bath with you – this may calm you both
❖ over-the-counter medication
❖ homeopathic remedies
❖ cranial osteopathy.

SUCKING
Windy and colicky babies like to suck, as this reduces pain. It provides a distraction and also helps the body to produce endorphins, which help to relieve pain naturally. Some babies like to suck on a dummy; others prefer their own or a parent's finger. As sucking offers temporary relief, some parents feed their babies very frequently, especially if breast-feeding. Once breast-feeding is established, stick to two- or three-hourly feeds to allow time for digestion. Cooled boiled water, from a spoon or a beaker, may help to bring up wind before a feed.

RESEARCH EVIDENCE
Research has found that colic can damage parent-baby relationships. Parents lose confidence as their efforts to soothe their colicky baby are fruitless. Because they feel inadequate, when their baby expresses a need, they respond with confusion rather than positive action. Massage can relieve colic temporarily, but it can also aid in breaking the cycle of ineffectuality, as parents feel their actions do, in some way, help their baby.

TECHNIQUES FOR PAIN RELIEF

There are various massage strokes (*see pages 80–81*) that may ease your baby's colic or help him to pass wind. Perform the strokes when he is not distressed, or at least, not too distressed. If lying on his back increases your baby's pain, place him on your lap, with his head by your knees and his feet by your hips, and raise your knees so he is lying at an angle. You can massage him with his clothes and nappy on, but you may achieve better results if he is naked. Wait for at least 30 minutes after a feed before you massage. The holding positions shown here may also bring temporary relief to babies with colic or wind.

HOLDING POSITIONS

BOUNCING YOUR BABY ON YOUR ARM
Stand with one arm outstretched and place your baby on your forearm, with his head nearest to your hand and his legs straddling your upper arm. Position your free hand firmly on his back to keep him steady. Press the heel of your lower hand into his abdomen, just below the ribs. Now bounce your outstretched arm up and down gently. This may relieve your baby's stomach pain and bring up wind.

CARRYING YOUR BABY UPRIGHT
Stand and hold your baby upright against your chest, facing outwards. Position one arm around him across his abdomen, below his ribs, to support his weight. Place your free hand over his nappy between the front of his thighs to help keep him balanced. Walk around, bouncing gently, or bounce on the spot. This may relieve pain in your baby's stomach and gut and bring up wind. You may find it easier to position his bottom on your hip so your arm does not support all his weight.

79

STROKES TO EASE COLIC AND WIND

1 ▼ MASSAGING THE SIDES OF THE ABDOMEN Position your baby on his back with his feet nearest to you. Place your hand on one side of his abdomen, fingers pointing downwards. Pull the flesh up towards the navel, then repeat the stroke with your other hand. Continue in this way, using both hands consecutively in a rhythmic action, then repeat on his other side. This helps to empty the stomach of its contents.

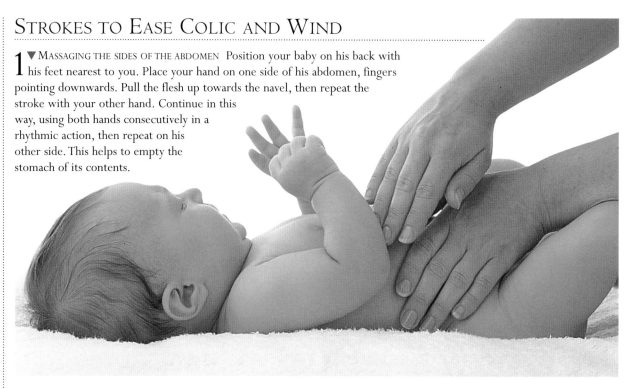

2 LITTLE CIRCLES AROUND THE NAVEL Hold the first two fingers of one hand together and place them next to your baby's navel. Press gently, making a circular motion, then release the pressure. Slide your fingers clockwise around the navel a few centimetres and repeat. Continue in this way, spiralling outwards until you reach the inside of your baby's right hip (see page 21). This stroke moves the contents of the small intestine along the gut. Working in a clockwise direction follows the natural flow of the gut.

3 LARGE CIRCLES AROUND THE ABDOMEN Place your hand on your baby's abdomen, just inside his right hip. Stroke up firmly with the flat of your fingers and your palm until you reach the right side of the rib cage. Leading with your fingers, stroke across the diaphragm to the same point on your baby's left side. Now stroke down to just inside his left hip, then across the base of the abdomen to the starting position (see page 21). Repeat several times. This stroke encourages the contents of the colon to move forwards.

4 ▼ CYCLING MOVEMENTS WITH THE LEGS Hold your baby's ankles and bend one knee up to his abdomen, then straighten the leg. As you pull it straight gently, bend his other knee up to his abdomen. Repeat this 'cycling' movement slowly and rhythmically a few times. This motion can help your baby to expel wind.

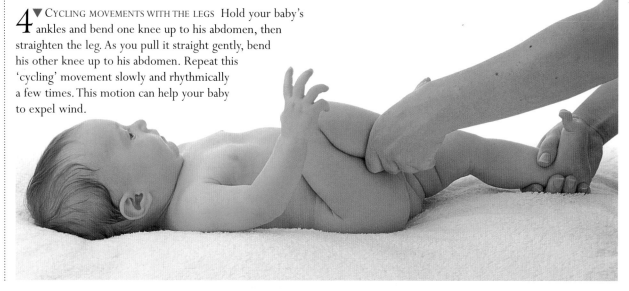

5 BENDING THE KNEES SIMULTANEOUSLY Take hold of your
baby's ankles, one in each hand. Bend both his legs to
bring his knees up to his abdomen. Hold his legs in this
position for a few seconds, then straighten
them gently. Repeat slowly several
times. This action may help to relieve
abdominal pain caused by wind.

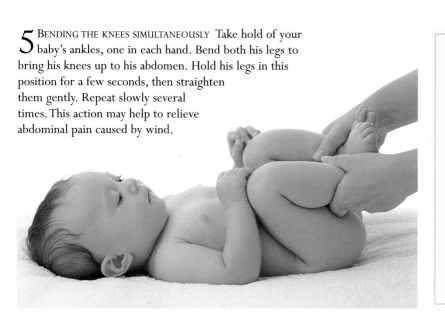

CASE HISTORY

"David got colic and cried a lot,
so I took him to a baby-massage
session at our local child health
clinic, hoping it would help. It
did. When I put him on the floor
to massage him, he immediately
cried. The maternal and child
health nurse showed me a way of
holding him on my forearm, with
my hand pressing into his stomach,
and when I did this, he stopped
crying at once. All the mothers,
myself included, were impressed.
I use this 'miracle cure' often
when David cries with colic now."

6 MASSAGING THE BASE OF THE SPINE Turn your baby over to lie on his front,
with his feet nearest to you. Place the heel of your hand in the dimple
just above the centre of his buttocks. Move the heel of your hand in
a clockwise direction, pressing gently. Repeat several times.
This stroke helps your baby to expel wind.

CONSTIPATION

❖

FROM TIME TO TIME, your baby may suffer from constipation. Massaging her abdominal area can be an effective way of both relieving and preventing this. The massage can be done when she is fully clothed, but is more effective if she is naked. Allow at least one hour after a feed before performing the strokes shown here. For this massage sequence, lie your baby on her back with her feet nearest to you.

COPING WITH CONSTIPATION

SIGNS AND SYMPTOMS

❖ NO STOOLS

A constipated child will frequently strain to pass a stool, but does not always achieve it.

❖ HARD STOOLS

When a stool is passed, it is hard, often resembling a solid pellet.

❖ CRYING

A hard stool can be painful to pass, so babies often cry just before and while passing a stool.

❖ TIME LAPSE BETWEEN STOOLS

If your child has not passed a stool for over three days, it is possible that she is constipated. It is normal for babies and young children to pass stools three times a day, and also normal not to 'go' at all for up to three days, and sometimes even longer if they are being breast-fed.

❖ STRAINING

Although it is a sign of constipation, 'straining' is not always a reliable indicator, as babies often go red in the face when pushing out a stool. If your child strains when passing a stool, then passes a soft, well-formed one, she is not constipated.

THINGS TO TRY

Besides abdominal massage, there are other options you should consider to relieve constipation or to prevent it from occurring:

❖ PLENTY OF FLUIDS

Make sure your baby is drinking enough fluids. Freshly-squeezed orange juice can help to move the bowels. Give your child two to four fluid ounces of diluted orange juice a day. Squeeze some oranges, strain the juice and dilute it to a ratio of one part orange juice to four parts boiled and cooled water.

❖ A HEALTHY DIET

Does your baby's diet include all she needs to prevent constipation? Up to four months, she should have breast or formula milk and juices. From four months, give her baby rice, cornmeal, pureed fruit and vegetables and stewed dried fruit. From six months, introduce cereals, pulses and grains gradually. Fibre and fluids help prevent constipation, but do not omit fat from the diet. Ask your maternal and child health nurse for advice if necessary.

❖ SENSIBLE ADVICE

Constipation can be a common problem with babies and young children. If it occurs, it tends to be recurring. Your doctor or maternal and child health nurse will be able to give you useful advice and support in coping with a constipated baby.

CASE HISTORY

"Rhian first became constipated when she started on solids. I tried giving her diluted orange juice as well as breast feeds, and stewed prunes and apricots, but nothing seemed to help. I found it very upsetting seeing her straining so much. Sometimes, she did not pass a stool for five or seven days. My sister massaged her children and offered to show me some strokes on the tummy which she felt might help. Amazingly, it worked! I would massage her tummy and then, when she started to strain, bend her knees up to her tummy and bring them back down again. I now use the massage each time Rhian is constipated, and also regularly to try and prevent it."

STROKES TO EASE CONSTIPATION

1 LITTLE CIRCLES AROUND THE NAVEL Place the first two fingers of one hand next to the navel. Press gently, making a circular motion, and release. Slide the fingers around the navel slightly and repeat. Work in a clockwise direction, spiralling outwards until you reach the right hip. This follows the flow of the small intestine, moving its contents along the gut.

2 LARGE CIRCLES AROUND THE ABDOMEN Starting just inside the right hip, move your flat fingers and palm up to the right side of the rib cage, then across to the same point on the left side. Stroke down to just inside the left hip, then along the base of the abdomen to the right hip. Repeat several times. This shifts the contents of the colon.

3 CYCLING MOVEMENTS WITH THE LEGS Hold your baby's ankles and bend one knee, bringing it up towards her abdomen. Now pull the leg gently until it is straight, and bend her other knee up to the abdomen as before. Repeat this 'cycling' motion slowly and rhythmically several times. This action may encourage a bowel movement.

4 BENDING THE KNEES SIMULTANEOUSLY Hold your baby's ankles and bend both her knees at the same time, bringing them up towards her abdomen. Hold her legs in this position for a few seconds, then pull them down gently until they are straight. Repeat slowly a number of times. This technique can help to open your baby's bowels.

FRACTIOUS CRYING

❖

BABIES CRY ON AVERAGE for two hours in every 24. Often, the cause of distress is obvious and easily remedied, but at other times, it can be unclear. Whatever the reason, if your baby cries, pick him up and cuddle him. The results of research studies indicate that the quicker a parent responds to a crying baby, the sooner the child stops crying. In some cases, nothing soothes screaming babies, which can be most frustrating for parents. Massage may calm your crying baby, but even if it does not, you could find that, between bouts of crying, both you and your baby enjoy massage and are relaxed by it.

COPING WITH A CRYING BABY

REASONS FOR DISTRESS
Typically, babies cry because they:
❖ are hungry
❖ need a nappy change
❖ desire a cuddle
❖ are tired and need to sleep
❖ want a change of position/scene
❖ are over-stimulated
❖ feel pain or seem uncomfortable.

THINGS TO TRY
❖ PHYSICAL CLOSENESS
Babies may be soothed by cuddling or rocking. Try talking or singing to your baby while holding him. You may feel it is wrong for your baby to fall asleep in your arms or be carried continuously, but do not worry about this – responding to his needs is more important.
❖ MOTION
Movement can be calming. Walk your baby around the house in your arms or a sling. Push him in a pram, put him in a rocking baby seat, or take him for a drive in a car.

❖ DISTRACTIONS
Try distracting your baby with a mobile, a musical toy, or a peep at the world through the window.
❖ BATHING
Water can be soothing, so try giving your baby a bath.
❖ HANDING HIM OVER
If you are tense, your baby might sense this and cry all the more. He may relax if he is held by someone else for a while, which also gives you a chance to rest.

INCONSOLABLE BABIES
If your baby cries for long, no matter what, and you do not know why, your confidence may be undermined and you may feel upset, frustrated and tired. If you feel angry with your baby for crying, or overwhelmed, put him in a safe place, such as his cot, and take a few minutes away from him to calm down. Do contact your doctor or maternal and child health nurse for advice.

RESEARCH EVIDENCE
Some parents may feel it is wrong to respond to a baby each time he cries, as this might 'spoil' him and give him unrealistic expectations of life. Recent research suggests that this point of view is counter-productive. The results of one study state that crying babies are soothed when lifted on to a caregiver's shoulder, and that they also become visually alert, showing that this attention is nurturing. Investigation into child psychology has established that by responding to a baby's needs, parents actually help to build his confidence (*see pages 72–73*). Nature also supports these theories: the same study reports that mothers are naturally compelled to attend to their crying babies and to stay close until they are calm. The study also found that mothers can distinguish a 'pain' cry from a less serious one. And it is also true that most adults want to 'do something' about a crying baby.

MASSAGE FOR FRACTIOUS BABIES

If your baby is accustomed to massage, you may be able to use it to help him calm down when he is crying. If he has not been massaged before, massage him a few times between bouts of crying to familiarize him with the strokes. Try using the strokes that you know he usually enjoys most of all. Effleurage strokes are soothing and reassuring, as they are long, firm and rhythmical. The strokes shown below concentrate on the abdomen and the back of the baby, but you can also try effleurage strokes on the front and back of the legs (*see* pages 22 and 31*), as well as on the arms (*see page 18*). If your baby continues to cry, stop the massage, wrap him in a towel to keep him warm, and pick him up. You may be able to massage him between bouts of crying, but do not try it if he becomes distressed.

Hold your baby to comfort him when he is crying, and try to distract him from his distress by singing a song or showing him a toy or colourful object

1 EFFLEURAGE STROKES DOWN THE ABDOMEN Position one hand across the abdomen, below the chest. Stroke down to the base of the abdomen, placing your other hand in the starting position as you do so. Just before the first hand lifts off, begin the stroke as before with the second hand. Repeat several times, with one hand always in contact with your baby's body.

2 EFFLEURAGE STROKES DOWN THE BACK Place one hand across the back, just below the neck, and stroke down until you reach the bottom. Place your other hand in the starting position before the first hand lifts off. Stroke down as before with the second hand. Repeat several times.

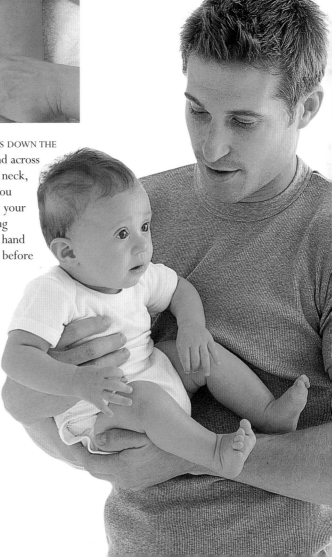

CASE HISTORY

"I took Laura to the crying clinic at four weeks. She had been crying almost continuously since she was two days old. By this time I was exhausted (she didn't sleep much) and at the end of my tether. The maternal and child health nurse came to see us at home. When Laura wasn't crying, she showed me how to perform a full-body massage on her. I could see almost instantly that Laura loved it. Now I massage her a few times a week, and when she cries — it usually calms her down. She is much happier these days, and sleeps better. I think the massage really helped her."

TEETHING

❖

MOST BABIES EXPERIENCE pain or discomfort when their teeth come through, as their gums become swollen. Massage helps because pressure can soothe swollen gums. The strokes shown here may ease your baby's teething pain temporarily, and encourage him to relax if he is fretful. Practise these strokes before teething begins if possible, so that your baby is familiar with them and allows you to perform them on him when his gums are uncomfortable. Also, try performing a full-body massage on your baby: this stimulates the production of endorphins in his body, which may help to alleviate pain.

RECOGNIZING TEETHING

SIGNS AND SYMPTOMS
Babies who are teething may:
❖ chew their fingers, or put them in their mouths
❖ have red cheeks
❖ experience a temperature
❖ suffer from red or inflamed gums
❖ have red skin in the nappy area.

CASE HISTORY
"I took Rebecca to baby-massage classes when she was six weeks old. A couple of the strokes the teacher showed us involved pressing the gums through the skin, above and below the lips. She said these strokes might ease teething pain. When Rebecca began teething, I tried those strokes. She enjoyed them and stopped being grizzly for a while afterwards, smiling and laughing again. I think they distracted her from the pain."

1 CIRCLES ON THE UPPER GUM LINE Place your thumbs next to each other on the dip above the top lip. Press gently with each thumb making a small, circular motion, then release the pressure. Move your thumbs outwards a little and repeat. Do this along the length of the upper lip, continuing along the top jaw line to the sides of the ears.

2 CIRCLES ON THE LOWER GUM LINE Position your thumbs next to each other just below the centre of your baby's lower lip. Press gently, making small circular movements with your thumb, then release. Slide your thumbs outwards a little way and repeat. Work along the length of the gum line in this way, then continue along the lower jaw line and up to the sides of the ears.

DRY SKIN

❖

SOMETIMES BABIES ARE BORN with dry, flaky skin on the face, hands, feet, or all over the body. In other cases, patches of dry skin develop over time, typically on the elbows, upper arms, nappy area or between the eyebrows. Regular oiling usually clears the problem and by massaging the oil in, you allow it to penetrate the skin deeply. Use a natural oil such as almond oil. Rub it into the affected area once or twice a day. If you are oiling your baby's face, avoid the eye area. Consult your doctor if the dry skin does not clear within a few days, or if it becomes red, inflamed, or worse in any way.

OILING YOUR CHILD'S SKIN

Olive, almond or grape-seed oil are good for dry skin. Place some on your hands, rub them together, and glide them over the affected area. Avoid oils that contain nut products, especially if there is a history of nut-allergy in your family. Dry skin may indicate sensitive skin, so watch for reactions to creams, soaps and detergents, and switch to a non-biological washing powder.

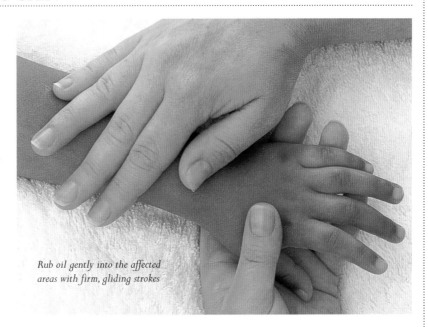

Rub oil gently into the affected areas with firm, gliding strokes

CASE HISTORY

"Daniel was a little overdue. When he was born, he had very dry skin all over his face and body. I was surprised at how scaly his skin was. My daughter also had dry skin when she was born, but not nearly as bad as Daniel's. I rubbed almond oil into his skin twice daily from when he was a few days old. I had already massaged my daughter, so I knew oil was good for dry skin. Daniel's skin soon became soft and velvety."

CRADLE CAP AND ECZEMA

Massaging a natural oil into the skin can relieve dry-skin conditions such as eczema and cradle cap. With cradle cap, massage a natural oil into the scalp daily, allowing the skin to absorb the oil. The dry skin eventually lifts away from the scalp. Brush it gently with your fingers, or run a comb through your baby's hair to help shift loosened dry skin. If your baby has eczema, massage oil into her skin to moisturize it. Do not massage the skin if it is broken, cracked, inflamed or very red. If you suspect your child has eczema, seek medical advice.

"*Massage* is simple in terms of *technique* yet powerful in what *it conveys*: your *love*, understanding, and *attention*"

QUESTIONS & ANSWERS

Q *Can I massage my baby when he has his clothes on?*

A Yes, particularly if he is newborn, if you feel both of you would like to be introduced to the massage strokes slowly. But do try and progress to removing his clothes. Children gain from any positive touch, but skin to skin contact – your bare hands against your baby's skin – is the most beneficial.

Q *Should I continue to massage my baby if he has a cold or fever?*

A Avoid massaging your child if he has a fever or cold. Many children do not want a massage when unwell, but enjoy lots of reassuring strokes and cuddles.

Q *If my child has a cut or a bruise, should I stop massaging her?*

A Avoid the bruised or cut area, which may be sore and painful to the touch. If your baby has a scar, do not massage the area until the scar has healed. But do continue to massage other areas of her body.

Q *My baby has eczema. Can I massage him?*

A Yes you can. Use a natural oil, such as olive or almond oil, to moisturize your baby's skin. Choose an organic oil if possible. If his skin is cracked or broken, do not massage the area until it has healed.

Q *Is massage recommended for asthmatic children?*

A An asthmatic child can benefit from massage, especially if the condition is stress or anxiety related. Massage may help her to relax, which could prevent asthma attacks or reduce their severity. Never massage your child during an attack, but do give her reassuring strokes on her arms, legs or head to help her feel less frightened.

Q *Can I use essential oils to massage my baby?*

A It is not advisable to use essential oils on babies or young children. Few essential oils are suitable, and those that are should be diluted in a base oil. Never use any essential oil on your child unless instructed by a trained aromatherapist.

Q *My child has very sensitive skin and is allergic to washing powders and soaps. Is it safe to use oil? What type of oil should I use?*

A A natural oil is much less likely to irritate sensitive skin than a synthetic variety. Select a light oil such as almond or apricot oil, choosing an organic variety if available. The more naturally the oil is produced, the better. Before using any oil, make sure you carry out a patch test on your child (*see page 15*) to ensure she is not sensitive to the oil you choose.

Q *My baby is allergic to nuts. Will she be affected if I massage her with a nut oil?*

A Do not use a nut oil under any circumstances as it may well affect your child. Try a natural oil such as grape-seed or olive oil. Some vegetable oils may contain nut products, so before using any oil, make absolutely certain that it is free of these. If the ingredients label is unclear, contact the manufacturer for further information. Once you have chosen an oil, make sure you perform a patch test on your baby (*see page 15*) to eliminate the possibility of sensitivity. If you have any doubts, massage your baby without oil – it is the loving touch you give her that is most important.

Q *My baby has recently had surgery. Is it safe to massage her?*

A Check with your surgeon before massaging your baby post-operatively. In many cases, once a child has recovered from surgery, massage is very beneficial to the baby and her parents. The touch is soothing to the child, and massaging their baby helps parents overcome anxieties about handling an infant in a delicate state. Avoid massaging the general area of the operation until the scar has healed – your doctor can give you more advice on this.

90

QUESTIONS & ANSWERS

Q *My baby often falls asleep when I massage her. Is this bad?*

A Some babies do fall asleep during massage, especially if snuggled up to their parent. This is fine until your baby is about four months old, after which time you should help her fall asleep with less and less physical contact, so she can put herself back to sleep when she wakes up in the night. If she is accustomed to falling asleep during massage, she is unlikely to go back to sleep alone.

Q *How can I tell if I'm using the right or wrong pressure for my massage strokes?*

A Your baby's skin will redden if the pressure is too firm. This is obvious on fair-skinned children, but be aware that it is less obvious on dark skin. If your child cries, pulls away or seems uncomfortable when you massage her, it may be that you are using too much pressure. Be aware of using too little pressure – this will give your child a tickling sensation. If you are unsure, use the pressure you would apply to rub cream into your face.

Q *I have just had a Caesarean. When can I start massaging my baby?*

A As soon as you feel you are able to. It may be hard to find a comfortable sitting position for massage, so keep the sessions short until your scar has healed.

Q *I have a bad back and find the massage positions on the floor uncomfortable. What should I do?*

A Your back pains may be caused by incorrect posture. When sitting on the floor, ensure you keep your back straight and bend forwards from the hips. Sitting on more cushions may help you to do this. If the floor is too uncomfortable, sit on a chair with a towel across your lap and your baby on the towel. Always keep one hand on your baby so she does not roll or slip off your lap. However, this position will not be safe once she is moving, rolling over or is too big for your lap.

Q *When I massage my young baby, my toddler becomes jealous. What can I do about this?*

A It is not unusual for a toddler to be jealous of a young sibling, especially if physical contact is involved. If your toddler would like to be massaged herself, make a regular time for it, when your baby is asleep or settled, so she feels she gets the same special attention from you as your baby does. Or ask her if she would like to 'help' you massage the baby. Show her how to rub oil gently into the baby's arms and legs, then praise her for doing it well. Perhaps she would enjoy massaging 'her baby' – a favourite teddy bear or doll – while you massage yours.

Q *I recently adopted a toddler. Can massage help us to bond?*

A Massage may certainly be one of the ways in which you establish a bond between you and your child. Before you begin, you must familiarize yourself with what the toddler does and does not like. Some children do not like to be touched, particularly by people they do not know well. Be warm, open and approachable. When he comes to you by himself, you will know that he is comfortable being close to you. At this point, start to touch him more and more. Stroke his hair, put your hand on his shoulder or an arm around him when you talk to him, especially if you are telling him what a good boy he is. Start to massage him when you feel confident that he can relax and enjoy it.

Q *My child is close to the end of her toddlerhood. Is there an age when I should stop massaging her?*

A The time to stop massaging your child is when she gives you the cue. If she seems to be losing interest and often wriggles, sits up, rolls over or walks away during massage; if she cries or asks you not to do it, then respect her wishes and stop. If she continues to enjoy it, massage her for as long as you like, even into adulthood – it can be a special time of closeness between you then, too.

INDEX

❖

RESOURCES AND USEFUL ADDRESSES

In Australia, government-funded Early Childhood Health Centres provide advice, information and support to all parents and carers with children from birth to the age of five. Early childhood health professionals will assist with breastfeeding concerns, postnatal depression, sleep problems and day-to-day parenting issues. They organise parent groups in local areas to help establish a support network. They can also refer you to community and specialist services. In New Zealand, the Royal New Zealand Plunket Society provides similar services.

Parent Line
ACT Tel: (02) 62 78 3995
NSW Tel: 132055
Vic Tel: 132289
Qld Tel: 1300 301300
SA Tel: 1300 364100
WA Tel: 1800 654432
These government-funded helplines give advice on family relationships and parenting, as well as referrals to health services and other resources in your area.

International Association of Infant Massage (Australia) Inc.
PO Box 288
Fairfield
Victoria 3078
Tel/Fax: (03) 9486-4667
Members run infant massage classes for parents and carers around Australia.

In New Zealand:
Peggy and Mike Dawson
PO Box 33997
Takapuna
Auckland
New Zealand
Tel: (09) 489-8796
Email:mike.peg.dawson@xtra.co.nz

Karitane Mothercraft Society
PO Box 241
Villawood NSW 2163
Tel: (02) 9794-1800 (office hours)
Tel: (02) 9794-1852 (24 hours)
Country areas Tel: 1800 677 961 (freecall)
Organisation dedicated to solving problems that affect new parents and their babies.

Birthing Rites Australia
2/10 Denison Street
Bondi Junction NSW 2022
Tel: (02) 9387-3615
These experienced childbirth educators hold a weekly postnatal support group. Topics covered include baby massage, breastfeeding and settling techniques. They provide information on independent midwives, osteopaths and massage and yoga facilities. Fees apply.

New Zealand Register of Osteopaths
22 Picton Street
Howick
Auckland
New Zealand
Tel: (09) 537-2518

Australian Osteopathic Association (AOA)
PO Box 242
Thornleigh
NSW 2120
Tel: (02) 9980-8511
Osteopathy can be beneficial to newborns and children with problems such as asthma, colic and recurrent ear infections, as well as for children with special needs.

The Royal New Zealand Plunket Society
PO Box 5474
Wellington
Tel: (04) 4710177
Plunket Karitane NZ
Tel: (04) 237 7152 (office hours)
Tel: 0800 933922 (Plunket Line) (midday to midnight)

REFERENCES

page 12

"...babies who are touched lovingly become ill and cry less often than those who are not."
Informed by
❖ G.S. Liptak, et al, 'Enhancing Infants' Development and Parent-Practitioner Interaction with Brazelton Neonatal Assessment Scale', **Pediatric**, July 1987, vol. 72, no. 1, p. 71–78.
❖ E.S. Haris, et al, 'Quality of Mother Infant Attachment and Pediatric Health Care Use', **Pediatric**, August 1989, vol. 84, no. 2, p. 248–54.
❖ D. Iwaniec et al, 'Helping Emotionally Abused Children who Fail to Thrive', **Early Prediction and Prevention of Child Abuse**, edited by K. Brown, et al, Wyley & Sons, 1991.
❖ S.K. Dihigo, 'New Strategies for the Treatment of Colic: Modifying the Parent/Infant Interaction', **The Journal of Pediatric Health Care**, 1998, vol. 12, no. 5, p. 256–62.
"A research study was carried out...with fathers and their babies..."
Informed by
❖ K. Scholz & C.A. Samuels, 'Neonatal Bathing and Massage Intervention with Fathers, Behavioural Effects 12 Weeks after Birth of the First Baby: The Sunraysia Australia Intervention Project', **International Journal of Behavioural Development**, 1992, vol.15, no.3, p. 67–81.

page 45

"...positive touch given in addition to routine handling..."

Informed by
❖ E. Lozoff et al, 'The Mother-Newborn Relationship: Limits of Adaptability', **The Journal of Pediatrics**, July 1997, vol. 99, no. 1, p. 1–12.
❖ L. Casler, 'The Effects of Extra-Tactile Stimulation of a Group of Institutionalised Infants', **Genealogy and Psychological Monograph**, 1965, vol. 71, p. 137–75. Cited in G. Westland (1993), 'Massage as a Therapeutic Tool: Part 1', **British Journal of Occupational Therapy**, vol. 56, no. 4, p. 129–34.

page 62

"...when premature babies receive routine care in hospital..."
Informed by
❖ J. White & R. LaBarba, 'The Effects of Tactile and Kinaesthetic Stimulation on Neonatal Development in the Premature Infant', **Developmental Psychology**, 1976, vol. 9, p. 569.
❖ D. Nelson, et al, 'Effects of Tactile Stimulation on Premature Infant Weight Gain', **Journal of Obstetric, Gynaecological and Neonatal Nursing**, May/June 1986, p. 262–67.
❖ T. Field, et al, 'Massage of Preterm Newborns to Improve Growth and Development', **Pediatric Nursing**, November/December 1987, vol. 1, no. 6, p. 385–87.
❖ R.C. White-Traut & M.B. Goldman, 'Premature Infant Massage – Is It Safe?', **Pediatric Nursing,** 1988, vol. 14, no. 4, p. 285–89

❖ L. Paterson, 'Baby Massage on the Neonatal Unit', **Nursing**, December 1990, vol. 4, no. 3, p. 19–21.

page 78

"...colic can damage parent-baby relationships."
Informed by
❖ S.K. Dihigo, 'New Strategies for the Treatment of Colic: Modifying the Parent/Infant Interaction', **The Journal of Pediatric Health Care**, 1998, vol. 12, no. 5, p. 256–62.

page 84

"...the quicker a parent responds to a crying baby..."
Informed by
❖ E. Lozoff et al, 'The Mother-Newborn Relationship: Limits of Adaptability', **The Journal of Pediatrics**, July 1997, vol. 99, no. 1, p. 1–12.
"...this point of view is counter-productive."
Informed by
❖ I. St. James-Roberts, et al, 'Stability and Outcome of Persistent Infant Crying'. **Infant Behaviour and Development**, 1998, vol. 21, no. 3, p. 411–35.
"...crying babies are soothed when lifted on to a caregiver's shoulder....mothers are naturally compelled to attend to their crying babies... mothers can distinguish a pain cry..."
Informed by
❖ E. Lozoff et al, 'The Mother-Newborn Relationship: Limits of Adaptability', **The Journal of Pediatrics**, July 1997, vol. 99, no. 1, p. 1–12.

ACKNOWLEDGMENTS

AUTHORS' ACKNOWLEDGMENTS
Nicki Bainbridge: I would like to thank Alan Heath; Sonia Prazeres, my baby-massage teacher; Jane Scofield, Meena Davis and Mary Magowan of Community Health South London; my clients, who have taught me much; my mother Rosemary Bainbridge for her faith in me, her enthusiasm and encouragement; my husband Richard Hatton for his love, support and flexibility; my children Daisy and Edward for their amenability while I wrote this book, and for teaching me so much about massage and touch; Ruth Bryan, Barbara and Graham Hatton for their help with child care; the team at Dorling Kindersley and all those who worked on the photo shoots, including Julie Fisher, whose fun, calm and relaxed manner resulted in beautiful pictures.
Alan Heath: For their help, support, patience, guidance and advice, I would like to thank Drs. Eve Rossor, Gill duMont and Aideen Naughton, and Annie Humphris, Jane Thorpe, Janet Abbot, Christine Prior, Geraldine Finney and Jane Schofield.

PUBLISHER'S ACKNOWLEDGMENTS
Dorling Kindersley would like to thank Nicola Cox and Conrad van Dyk for DTP design work, Sue Carlton for the index, Clare Hacking for proofreading, Mark Weyman, and Habitat and PHP (Perfectly Happy People) for providing props.
Models Melanie and Jason Ashenden, Robina Aslam and Sophia Maria O'Reilly, Nicki Bainbridge, Georgie Caine, Allen and Tanis Clarke, Ziz and Zoe Chater, Carey Combe and Cordelia Hawkins, Arden Devine, Mysanwy and Chen Dew, Lee-Ann and Amirah Edwards, Thor and Jasper Haley, Donna Harding and Star Epiphany, Margarita Foncenada and Gabriella Grant-Foncenada, Lisa Greenspan and Silas Parker, Ophelia Jackson, Michele, Kamilah and Tariq Jogee, Jeremy, Spencer and Ellis Roots, Isobel Stewart, Claire Trotman and Jasmine Graham, Jackie Vanhorne and Shannon Vanhorne-Quartey, Tomos Vaughan-Streater and Johnathan Ward.
Make-up Artists Amanda Clarke and Elizabeth Burridge.
Additional Photography p. 6, 50, 66, 76, Liz McAulay.

ACKNOWLEDGMENTS